EAST MEETS SOUTHWEST

INNOVATIVE CUISINE FROM SANTACAFÉ

EAST MEETS SOUTHWEST

BY MICHAEL FENNELLY

WITH A FOREWORD BY JAMES BIBO

PHOTOGRAPHY BY CHARLES GREER

CHRONICLE BOOKS · SAN FRANCISCO

PRINTED in Hong Kong

LIBRARY OF CONGRESS CATALOGING IN PUBLICATION DATA
Fennelly, Michael.
    East meets Southwest / Michael Fennelly ; with an intro-
duction by James Bibo ; photography by Charles Greer.
     p.   cm.
    Recipes.
    Includes index.
    ISBN 0–87701–641–0
    1. Cookery, American—Southwestern style.   2. Cookery,
Oriental.   3. Santacafé (Restaurant : Santa Fe, N.M.)   I. Title.
TX715.2.S69F46   1991
641.5'09789'56—dc20   90–48041
                              CIP

BOOK AND COVER DESIGN: Michael Fennelly and Eleanor Caponigro
COVER PHOTOGRAPH: Charles Greer
TYPESETTING: Michael and Winifred Bixler

DISTRIBUTED in Canada by Raincoast Books,
112 East Third Avenue, Vancouver, B.C. V5T 1C8

10 9 8 7 6 5 4 3 2

CHRONICLE BOOKS
275 Fifth Street
San Francisco, California 94103

CONTENTS

FOR FRANK

ACKNOWLEDGEMENTS

It is not humanly possible to properly acknowledge all the help that has made this book come into being. Of the many that helped, here are only a few:

Many of the fresh baby vegetables and flowers, including the seven different kinds of Japanese squash seen on the title page, exist because of Elizabeth Berry, whose persistent and inspired work at her Gallina Canyon ranch is a continual gift to us all.

Howard Jacobsen gave invaluable counseling at the inception of this book. At Chronicle Books, David Barich approved the original concept, and, without his trust, there would be no book. Lisa Howard, Karen Pike, and Mary Ann Gilderbloom were amazingly patient and helpful during the many stages of this project.

As for the wonderful design of the book, we are indebted to Eleanor Morris Caponigro for her vast knowledge of book design, typography, and for her creative, expeditious perseverance.

Photographer Charles Greer's assistant Lynn Lown cleaned out the small refrigerator where he kept film so that we could store the perishables to be photographed that day, as well as enabling us to set up camp cooking facilities in his studio. Sylvia Souza organized, typed and deciphered pages of often illegible recipes for the manuscript.

For the numerous influences on my cooking, many good friends and peers need to be recognized, especially Julia Wagner, Walter Nicholls, Barbara Tropp, Jane Fennelly, and Rosanna and Steven Ottenstein.

Many of the Santacafé kitchen staff were instrumental in the preparation, writing and ideas seen here, in particular Gina Ziluca, Linda Stratton-Graczyk, Larry McGrael, and pastry chef Stephanie Morris, whose delightful desserts are featured in the final chapter.

For all the wonderful, diverse plates and props you see on these pages, thank you to Nancie Greer, Harriett Bibo, Forrest Moses, Japonesque, Mineo Mizuna, Romona Sakiestewa, Roddy Burdine, John Lightfoot, and DeWayne Youts.

Finally, it is the management team, staff, and customers of the Santacafé that have indefatigably shaped, changed, cajoled, whined, obsessed, rebelled, ranted, raved, requested, demanded, counseled, praised, critiqued, liked, disliked, labored, loved, and generously given of themselves—literally hundreds of thousands of you through the years. Thank you all.

Santacafé is known for its innovative blending of the Asian with the New Mexican, for being a restaurant where the East successfully meets the Southwest. Chef Michael Fennelly's kitchen has created scores of dishes that are distinguished by their original use of local ingredients and their sometimes studied, sometimes whimsical presentations.

On a 1987 trip to Japan, Mike and I were at first hard-pressed to uncover the essence of the East that we were so eager to explore. But that quickly changed. One morning at 4:00 A.M., in the food stalls of the big Tokyo fish market, we found ourselves without any language but sign language and eagerly pointing to whatever others were eating. Soon we were downing plates of raw fish and bowls of sublimely flavored broth. We had finally tapped into the culinary mysteries of Asia. This somewhat unconventional approach to discovery continues to fuel our basic attitude toward food.

From that trip we learned that the culinary marriage of Asia and the American Southwest is rooted in the similarity of their rich heritages. A respect for the ancient past and a strong identification with place characterizes these geographically distant lands. They both possess gentle yet powerful landscapes and a profound respect for the unique qualities that define each season.

Crosscultural cooking, which became a national trend in the late eighties, has elicited mixed reviews from the nation's food writers. Michael Fennelly's cuisine, however, stands apart from any momentary culinary fashion. His constantly evolving palette continuously leads him on a path of investigation. Many dishes that appear in these pages led several lives before they took on their present guises. They have been tested and retested, adapted and transformed, some of them over many years.

East Meets Southwest takes the reader, whether he or she is a home cook who intends to prepare these inspired dishes or a browser who wants only to explore the visual artistry, on a culinary adventure from conception through execution to presentation. Some readers may want to use the book to re-create exactly what is pictured; others may prefer to admire the beautifully arranged presentations and then create a dish that reflects a more personal statement. Although the photographs were carefully composed, Mike's spontaneous, last-minute addition or deletion from a plate is part of his culinary genius.

The kitchen where this experimentation takes place is in my restaurant, the nobly handsome Santacafé, a 180-year-old triple-adobe Spanish colonial courtyard house that is at once both formal and casual. This same eclecticism is the hallmark of Michael Fennelly's cooking. What you find in these pages will be equally appropriate for a picnic or a state dinner. Bon appétit.

JAMES BIBO

The very small seaport town of Northport, New York, is where my cooking adventures began. I grew up in the sixties when fresh fish and shellfish were readily available from the then-unpolluted Long Island Sound. In those days we ate lots of simply prepared seafoods—clams grilled over hot coals, mountains of steamed shrimp—and it is this simplicity that I still strive for in my cooking.

At a young age I became fascinated with the Orient, particularly Japan. It was a time of great discovery for me, and I sought out Asian foods, even though tiny Northport was a very limited marketplace.

My stepmother, Jane, was a good role model. She had a knack for cooking, but didn't feel the need to spend hours in the kitchen preparing a meal. Jane worked with the same uncomplicated ease, using primarily local ingredients, that distinguishes the best Asian cooking.

I studied art at Parson's School of Design in New York City, and while living in Manhattan I explored almost every ethnic cuisine imaginable. I tasted sushi for the first time at one of those conveyor-belt establishments. The place became my favorite haunt. During those years I also developed my own design style. It was one of minimalist expression executed through hard lines and organic forms; it reduced any given composition to its most essential components. This uncomplicated, unpretentious style has carried over into my cooking.

After college I moved to northern California, where a new cuisine was evolving that reminded me of what I had eaten as a child. It was a straightforward approach to cooking that used foods indigenous to the region and prepared them quickly and without fuss. In just a short time, I was incorporating these trends into my own culinary ideas, which favored Asian tastes. At this point I began combining the flavors of the East and the West. I made my first of thousands of Chinese dumplings, experimenting with every possible blend of ingredients for the fillings. I learned to prepare sushi, viewing it as a vehicle for countless variations.

The artist in me was drawn to New Mexico for its sheer physical beauty. I had never before seen a place in the United States with such a unique combination of "ingredients," a place where land, sky, and architecture formed an almost mystical union. I immediately felt the excitement of discovery and a deep sense of history. The East and West coasts had always made me think of lush landscapes; New Mexico epitomized a very different extreme. I was captivated by the rawness of the terrain, the sparse vegetation, and the innate simplicity that defines pure Southwest style.

A combination of this Southwest simplicity and the refined minimalism of the Orient is at the heart of my cooking. At Santacafé I often marry New Mexican and Asian ingredients, such as in the maki rolls filled with trout and chiles on page 66.

I have found that by employing Japanese cooking styles, ingredients, and presentations I can give traditional New Mexican dishes a subtlety seldom found in Southwest cuisine. The result is a truly provocative East-West table that relies on foods in their purest forms and mixes them in unexpected ways.

East Meets Southwest presents my personal sense of food—its taste and style. Although some of the recipes have no obvious East-West identity, they all reflect an East-West sensibility. The way a chive intersects the rim of a plate, or a waterfall of broken wontons cascades in the Asian Napoleon (page 80) brings to mind the Japanese idea of *wabi*, or perfection in spontaneous imperfection.

Cooking is an art form in which foods need only a delicate transformation to create an outstanding dish. I am a firm believer that what we eat should always look and taste like what it is. There are no roses made out of tomatoes or complex sauces in this book. The recipes emphasize taste, ease of preparation, and a presentation that respects reductionist beauty.

The book is organized into three sections: To Begin, To Continue, and To End. In the first section you will find salads, sushi, soups, and other dishes that can open a meal or can stand alone as a light lunch or a late-night supper. To Continue contains more substantial fare, dishes that are suitable for serving after an appetizer or as satisfying meals on their own. To End brings together an array of irresistible desserts that are perfect finales to a meal or can be enjoyed as sweet interludes any time of the day.

It is my hope that everyone who uses this book will come away with a new vision of food—an understanding of its beauty when it is presented in its purest form.

I challenge you not to be afraid of food, to feel confident about mixing together almost whatever you'd like, and, most importantly, to be spontaneous and to have fun.

MICHAEL FENNELLY

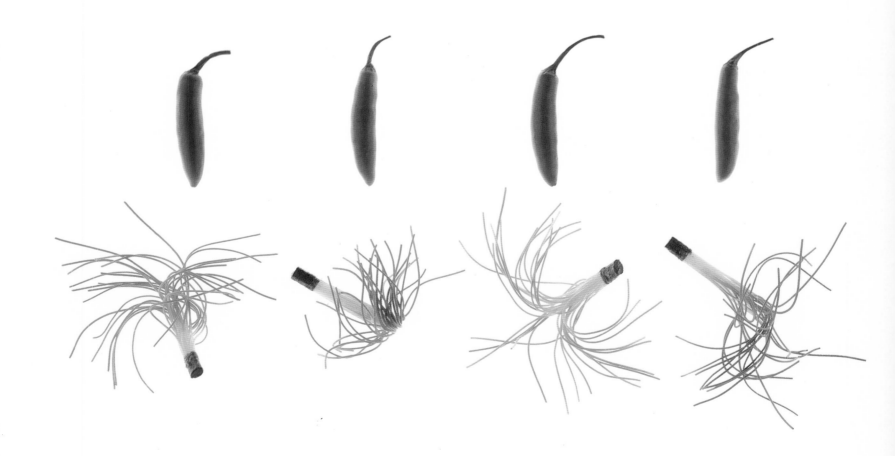

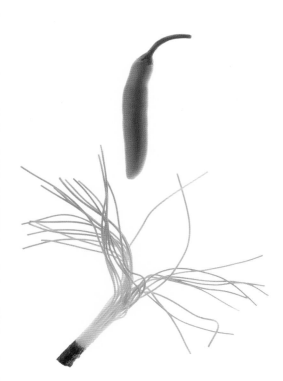

1 piece (12 ounces) filet mignon, frozen for at least
   2 hours or until solid enough to facilitate slicing
Zest of 2 lemons, cut in long, thin strips, for
   garnish
40 leaves fresh cilantro, for garnish
1 fresh poblano or Anaheim chile, roasted, peeled,
   seeded, deribbed, and julienned, for garnish

ORANGE-LIME SAUCE

¼ cup fresh orange juice
¼ cup fresh lime juice
¼ cup Thai fish sauce
1½ tablespoons sugar
1 teaspoon ground Chimayo or other medium-hot
   dried red chile
4 cloves garlic, chopped
1 teaspoon ketchup
2 tablespoons olive oil
Pinch cayenne pepper
Pinch salt

A citrus-based sauce adds a tropical touch to this exotic first course. Serve with thinly sliced, crusty French bread.

On an electric slicer or with a sharp knife, cut the frozen beef against the grain into 1/16-inch-thick slices. As the slices are cut, place them between sheets of waxed paper to keep them separated. Alternatively, ask your butcher to slice the meat on an electric slicer.

To make the sauce, in a food processor or blender combine all the ingredients. Blend for 3 minutes. Set aside.

On each of 4 to 6 plates, arrange a thin layer of the beef slices. Lightly drizzle the sauce over the beef and garnish with lemon zest, cilantro, and julienned chile. Serve immediately.

SERVES *4 to 6.*

3 small heads Baby Red or Young Green romaine
   lettuce (see Note)

½ teaspoon ground medium-hot dried red chile

1 teaspoon finely chopped fresh cilantro

½ teaspoon kosher salt

2 cloves garlic, finely chopped

2 tablespoons olive oil

1 loaf French bread, cut into small cubes

½ cup freshly grated Parmesan cheese, for garnish

1 can (2 ounces) anchovy fillets, drained, for garnish

CAESAR DRESSING

Juice of 1 large lemon

1 tablespoon finely minced garlic

1 tablespoon Dijon-style mustard

1½ tablespoons red wine vinegar

2 teaspoons Worcestershire sauce

7 dashes Tabasco sauce

½ teaspoon kosher salt

1 teaspoon freshly ground black pepper

1 can (2 ounces) anchovy fillets, drained and
   minced

1½ cups olive oil

4 egg yolks

Here is a classic, updated with the addition of chile-laced croutons.

Preheat the oven to 375° F. Separate the romaine leaves, discarding the tough outer leaves; refrigerate. In a medium-sized bowl, combine the ground chile, cilantro, salt, garlic, and oil. Gently toss the cubed bread in this mixture, then turn out onto a baking sheet, spreading the cubes out in a single layer. Bake, turning occasionally to brown evenly, until golden brown and crispy, about 15 minutes. Cool and reserve.

To make the dressing, in a medium-sized bowl combine the lemon juice, garlic, mustard, vinegar, Worcestershire, Tabasco, salt, pepper, and anchovies. Lightly whisk to blend. Continuing to whisk, slowly drizzle in olive oil, adding just enough to form a smooth emulsion. Whisk in egg yolks. Taste and correct seasoning.

Just before serving, place chilled lettuce leaves and as many croutons as desired in a large wooden bowl. Add dressing, a little at a time, and toss gently, coating leaves evenly. Garnish with Parmesan, anchovy fillets, and additional croutons.

SERVES *8.*

NOTE: *When purchasing lettuce for this salad, choose the choicest and most petite heads. Look for these small-leaf varieties in specialty-produce stores and better supermarkets.*

1 pound lean fresh tuna fillet, frozen for at least
  4 hours or until solid enough to facilitate slicing
1 cup mayonnaise
2 tablespoons prepared *wasabi*
$\frac{1}{4}$ cup *gari*
6 green onions, cut into 2$\frac{1}{2}$-inch lengths and finely
  julienned
2 tablespoons sesame seed, toasted
2 fresh jalapeño chiles, seeded, deribbed, and
  finely minced

Today the choices for carpaccio *run the gamut from traditional beef to duck or venison. Tuna is my favorite, however. It's light and airy, and in this version is enhanced by the sharpness of the* wasabi. *The* gari, *or "pickled ginger," delivers a refreshing counterpoint to the other flavors.*

On an electric slicer or with a sharp knife, cut the frozen tuna against the grain into $\frac{1}{16}$-inch-thick slices. As the slices are cut, arrange them in a single layer on each of 8 individual serving plates.

In a small bowl, mix together the mayonnaise and wasabi. *Attractively garnish each serving of tuna with 3 stripes of* wasabi *mayonnaise and several pieces of* gari. *Sprinkle with green onions, sesame seed, and jalapeño.*

SERVES *8*.

7 Japanese eggplants, trimmed and cut lengthwise
　　into $\frac{1}{4}$-inch-thick slices

3 tablespoons olive oil

2 cloves garlic, chopped

$\frac{1}{2}$ teaspoon kosher salt

$\frac{1}{2}$ teaspoon freshly ground black pepper

POBLANO-GINGER-LIME BUTTER

$\frac{1}{2}$ pound unsalted butter, softened

2 tablespoons finely minced fresh poblano chile, or
　　I tablespoon finely minced fresh jalapeño chile

2 tablespoons finely minced fresh ginger

2 tablespoons fresh lime juice

I tablespoon freshly grated lime zest

I teaspoon salt

I teaspoon freshly ground white pepper

The trick to this recipe is not to overcook the eggplant. You may need to adjust the cooking time slightly, depending upon your oven. The eggplant should be cooked through but still firm and it should be barely crisp on the outside. Any leftover butter may be refrigerated or frozen for future use.

Preheat the oven to 400°F. Place the eggplant in a medium-sized bowl and toss with oil, garlic, salt, and black pepper. Place eggplant on a baking sheet and cover with aluminum foil. Roast for 10 minutes. Uncover and continue to roast for an additional 5 minutes. The eggplant should be slightly browned and just tender.

While the eggplant is cooking, combine all the ingredients for the butter in a food processor and process until well combined and smooth, about 2 minutes. Alternatively, combine all the ingredients in a medium-sized mixing bowl and beat until smooth. Let stand at room temperature until ready to serve the eggplant.

To serve, place a small dollop of the butter on each eggplant slice.

SERVES *4.*

1 package (1 pound) square wonton wrappers

4 egg whites, lightly beaten

3 quarts chicken stock

1 small red bell pepper, seeded, deribbed, and finely julienned, for garnish

10 nasturtium leaves, for garnish (optional)

WONTON FILLING

1 roasted chicken (3½ pounds), at room temperature

½ teaspoon grated fresh ginger

1 bunch spinach (about ¾ pound), trimmed and cut into ¼-inch-wide strips

5 eggs, lightly scrambled and cooled

2 small shallots, finely minced

1 tablespoon Asian sesame oil

1 tablespoon soy sauce

½ teaspoon kosher salt

¼ teaspoon hot-pepper flakes

In New Mexico the growing season is short, so whenever I have the chance I use fresh nasturtiums in the kitchen. The leaves are peppery in flavor, and when they are floated on a soup they look like water-lily pads. You will need to have a whole roasted chicken on hand to make the filling.

To make the filling, remove meat from cooled roasted chicken. Coarsely chop meat into ¼-inch chunks. In a large bowl, combine the chicken, ginger, about three fourths of the spinach, eggs, shallots, sesame oil, soy sauce, salt, and pepper flakes. Toss to mix well.

To assemble wontons, lay out 6 to 8 wrappers at a time. With a fingertip, lightly moisten the edge of each wrapper with egg white. Place a spoonful of filling in the center of each wrapper. Fold wrapper over to form a rectangle; press edges together to seal. Crimp wrapper along the sealed long edge to form a pouch shape. As wontons are formed, place them on a lightly floured baking sheet. Repeat until all filling is used. Refrigerate wontons until you are ready to cook them.

Bring the chicken stock to a boil in a large pot. Gently drop in wontons, adding only as many as the pot will hold without crowding. Return to a gentle boil. Reduce heat to medium and simmer until wontons float and are cooked through, 3 to 5 minutes. Remove to a large bowl and cover until all wontons are cooked.

Ladle hot stock and wontons into serving bowls. Garnish with bell pepper, reserved spinach, and nasturtium leaves.

SERVES *10.*

$3\frac{1}{3}$ cups short-grain white rice

4 cups water

6 tablespoons seasoned rice vinegar

$\frac{1}{2}$ pound lean fresh tuna fillet

10 snow peas, trimmed

6 large domestic mushrooms, stemmed

6 jumbo shrimp, cooked, shelled, and deveined

1 thin omelet made with 4 eggs, cooled to room
   temperature

3 snow crab legs, cooked and shelled

1 large carrot, peeled, blanched, and chilled

30 fresh *enoki* mushrooms

1 fresh Anaheim chile, roasted and peeled

1 cup well-drained, chopped, steamed spinach
   (about 1 pound uncooked)

3 tablespoons prepared *wasabi*

$\frac{1}{2}$ cup tamari

$\frac{1}{2}$ cup *gari*

*For a true East-West feast, serve this colorful sushi platter with
Shrimp-Filled Dumplings with Serrano Chile Dipping Sauce (page 36)
and Spring Rolls with 3-Chile Dipping Sauce (page 46).*

*In a heavy-bottomed, medium-sized pot, combine the rice and water.
Cover, place over medium heat, and bring to a boil. Raise heat to high,
and boil for 2 minutes. Reduce heat to medium and cook for 5 minutes.
Reduce heat to low and cook for 15 minutes or until all water has been
absorbed. Turn heat off and let rice stand, covered, for an additional
13 minutes. Do not uncover pot even to peek. To prepare rice in a rice
cooker, follow manufacturer's instructions.*

*Using a rice paddle or flat wooden spoon, spread the hot rice in a
thin layer in a shallow wood or plastic vessel. Sprinkle with 4 tablespoons of the vinegar and gently turn the rice with horizontal cutting
strokes. At the same time, cool the rice quickly and thoroughly to room
temperature with a hand fan or an electric fan. When cool, cover rice
with a damp cloth. Do not refrigerate. The rice will keep for up to
7 hours at room temperature.*

*To prepare toppings, begin by chilling the tuna in the freezer for
20 minutes. Combine the snow peas and 1 tablespoon of the vinegar in a
small bowl and let stand 1 hour. Combine the domestic mushrooms and
the remaining 1 tablespoon vinegar in another bowl and let stand for
1 hour. Split the shrimp in half lengthwise and reserve. Cut the omelet
into thin strips and reserve. Cut each crab leg into 3 equal pieces and
reserve. Slice the carrot ⅛ inch thick on the diagonal. Cut ¾ inch off
the base of each* enoki *mushroom. Seed and derib the chile, then slice
lengthwise into thin strips. Combine the* enoki *mushrooms and chile
strips in a small bowl and toss well. Place the spinach in a small bowl.
Cut the chilled tuna against the grain into slices about ⅛ inch thick.*

*Line a large plate, platter, or shallow bowl with a ¾-inch-deep layer
of the reserved rice. Spread a very thin layer of* wasabi *over the rice.
Beginning at one end, place tuna slices over rice, overlapping them
slightly. Working your way across the tuna layer, arrange the prepared
ingredients in rows over the tuna in the following order: carrot, snow
peas, shrimp, omelet strips, crab,* enoki *mushrooms and chile, tuna,
spinach, and domestic mushrooms. As you work, overlap the ingredients
slightly. Serve with tamari and* gari *on the side.*

SERVES *6.*

1 duck (4½ pounds)

1 tablespoon kosher salt

1 bunch watercress

1 bunch arugula

1 head butter lettuce

2 Belgian endives

1 head radicchio

1 pint raspberries, for garnish

ROASTED SHALLOT VINAIGRETTE

¼ cup sherry vinegar

6 shallots, roasted and chopped (see Note)

1 teaspoon salt

½ teaspoon freshly ground black pepper

1 cup virgin olive oil

1½ tablespoons walnut oil

Succulent duck meat and fragrant fresh raspberries are perfectly matched in this elegant salad.

Preheat the oven to 450°F. Rinse the duck with cold water and pat dry with paper towels. Rub duck, including cavity, with salt. Place duck, breast side up, on a rack in a roasting pan and roast until golden brown, about 1½ hours. The duck should be cooked medium-rare. Let cool, then carve meat from carcass. Cut meat into thin strips and reserve.

Tear the watercress, arugula, and butter lettuce into bite-sized pieces. Cut off bottom ½ inch of endive heads and separate leaves. Separate the radicchio leaves; tear into bite-sized pieces if large. Set greens aside.

To make the vinaigrette, combine the vinegar, shallots, salt, and pepper in a bowl. Slowly whisk in the oils. Taste and correct seasonings.

Combine all prepared greens and duck in a large salad bowl. Add just enough salad dressing to coat all ingredients generously; reserve remaining dressing for another use. Toss well. Garnish with raspberries.

SERVES 4.

NOTE: *To roast shallots, place in a preheated 450°F oven for 15 minutes. Cool and peel.*

4 boneless chicken breast halves
   (about 4 ounces each)

¼ cup dry sherry

¼ cup olive oil

¼ teaspoon kosher salt

¼ teaspoon freshly ground black pepper

2 carrots, peeled and finely julienned

30 snow peas, trimmed and finely julienned

2 red bell peppers, seeded, deribbed, and finely
   julienned

4 stalks celery, trimmed and finely julienned

1 head red or green leaf lettuce, cut crosswise
   into 1-inch-wide strips

6 cups peanut oil, for deep-frying

1 package (8 ounces) bean thread noodles
   (see Note)

2 tablespoons sesame seed, toasted, for garnish

SPICY TOMATO DRESSING

2 cups tomato paste

4 cloves garlic

3 shallots

1 tablespoon chopped red onion

1 tablespoon chopped fresh cilantro

½ teaspoon ground Sichuan peppercorns

1 tablespoon ground medium-hot dried red chile

½ cup seasoned rice vinegar

½ cup firmly packed brown sugar

½ cup Asian sesame oil

½ cup olive oil

2 tablespoons grated fresh ginger

¼ teaspoon cayenne pepper

¼ cup granulated sugar

¾ cup bottled teriyaki sauce

½ cup soy sauce

Juice of 2 lemons

Some time ago at a Korean restaurant in Los Angeles, I had a sashimi salad with an outstanding red dressing. I created this sauce in an attempt to duplicate it. It comes close to the original and tastes great on chicken, beef, or fish. Store the unused dressing in a covered jar in the refrigerator for up to seven days.

Prepare a fire in a charcoal grill. In a medium-sized bowl, combine the chicken, sherry, olive oil, salt, and black pepper. Turn the chicken to coat thoroughly. Grill the chicken over medium-hot coals, turning occasionally to prevent charring, until cooked through, about 7 minutes. Cool, cut into thin strips, and reserve. Prepare the vegetables; reserve.

In a medium-sized saucepan, heat the peanut oil to 375° F, or until a bean thread noodle dropped into it puffs up and floats to the surface immediately. Pull the noodles apart into small bunches. Drop a bunch into the oil. When it puffs and turns white, turn it over to ensure even cooking. Remove with a slotted utensil to paper towels to drain. Repeat with the remaining noodles.

To make the dressing, combine the tomato paste, garlic, shallots, onion, and cilantro in a food processor or blender. Process 30 seconds. Add the Sichuan pepper, chile, vinegar, brown sugar, sesame oil, olive oil, ginger, cayenne, and granulated sugar. Process 1 minute. Add the remaining ingredients; process 2 minutes. Reserve.

In a medium-sized bowl, combine the reserved chicken, carrots, snow peas, bell peppers, and celery. Add just enough of the sauce to coat the chicken and vegetables lightly and toss gently to mix well. On a serving platter, arrange a layer of crispy noodles and then a layer of the reserved lettuce strips. Top with a layer of the chicken-vegetable mixture and garnish with toasted sesame seed.

SERVES *4.*

NOTE: *These thin, clear noodles, which are also called glass or cellophane noodles, can be found in Asian grocery stores and well-stocked supermarkets.*

$\frac{1}{4}$ cup fresh orange juice

$\frac{3}{4}$ cup fresh lime juice

I cup olive oil

2 pounds fresh bay scallops

$\frac{3}{4}$ cup finely minced red onion

$\frac{1}{2}$ cup minced green onions, including some green
tops

$\frac{1}{4}$ cup minced red bell pepper

$\frac{1}{4}$ cup fresh cilantro leaves, chopped

3 tablespoons minced, roasted and peeled fresh
Anaheim chile

2 teaspoons kosher salt

I teaspoon ground Sichuan peppercorns

Fresh cilantro leaves, for garnish

I teaspoon hot-pepper flakes, for garnish

Zest of 2 oranges, cut into threads with a zester,
for garnish

As a child in Southampton, Long Island, I gathered fresh bay scallops, dislodging them from just under the surface of the sand with my feet. One of the best ways to prepare the succulent, translucent white flesh of the scallop is to marinate it for ceviche. Seek out the very freshest scallops for this dish.

Combine the orange juice, lime juice, and olive oil in a large bowl. Pat the scallops dry with paper towels and add to bowl with the red onion, green onion, bell pepper, chopped cilantro, Anaheim chile, salt, and ground Sichuan peppercorns. Toss gently, cover, and refrigerate for 4 to 6 hours.

Transfer scallop mixture to a large serving bowl. Garnish with whole cilantro leaves, pepper flakes, and orange zest.

SERVES 6.

DOUGH

3 cups all-purpose flour

1½ teaspoons salt

1½ cups water, or as needed

2 teaspoons sugar

2 teaspoons active dry yeast

2 tablespoons black poppy seed

EGG WASH

2 eggs

½ cup milk

These crunchy sticks are easy to make and are good with just about anything. Although the recipe yields a large batch, don't worry about leftovers. You won't be able to stop eating them.

To make the dough by hand, combine the flour and salt in a large bowl. Make a well in the center and add the 1½ cups water, sugar, and yeast. With a fork, gradually combine these ingredients. Continue to stir, gradually working in flour, until mixture forms a mass that holds together. Add a little more water as needed for proper consistency.

To make the dough in a food processor, combine the flour and salt in the processor bowl. With the machine running, gradually add the sugar, yeast, and the 1½ cups water. Continue to process until mixture forms a mass that holds together, adding a little more water as needed for proper consistency.

Turn dough out onto a lightly floured board and knead until smooth, about 4 to 5 minutes. Dough should be firm and not sticky. Form into a smooth ball, cover with plastic wrap, and refrigerate for 1 hour.

To make the egg wash, in a small bowl whisk together eggs and milk; reserve.

To roll out the dough by hand, lightly flour a work surface and work with only a small portion of dough at a time. Roll out each portion, using as few strokes as possible and dusting with flour as necessary to prevent sticking, until sheet is ¼ inch thick. Dust the rolled-out dough with flour and let it rest for about 10 minutes. Then cut the sheet into ¾-inch-wide strips. Repeat with the remaining dough.

To roll out the dough on a pasta machine, follow the manufacturer's instructions and work with only a small portion of dough at a time. Put the dough through the rollers several times until the sheet is ¼ inch thick. Dust the sheet with flour if dough starts to become too sticky. Cut the sheet into ⅜-inch-wide strips. Repeat with the remaining dough.

Preheat the oven to 375° F. Lightly grease 2 baking sheets. Space dough strips ½ inch apart on the prepared baking sheets. Cut strips into 8-inch lengths. Brush with reserved egg wash. Sprinkle with poppy seed. Bake until golden, about 12 to 14 minutes. Cool on wire racks and store in an airtight container at room temperature.

MAKES *about 4 dozen breadsticks.*

1 tablespoon unsalted butter

1 pound shrimp, peeled and coarsely chopped

2 teaspoons grated fresh ginger

½ cup well-drained, chopped, cooked spinach
   (about ½ pound uncooked)

1 egg, lightly beaten

1 teaspoon Asian sesame oil

1 teaspoon cornstarch, dissolved in 1 tablespoon
   water

Pinch cayenne pepper

2 tablespoons chopped fresh cilantro

½ teaspoon salt

1 cup tamari or soy sauce

3 tablespoons Asian chile oil (see Note)

2 fresh serrano chiles, seeded, deribbed, and chopped

1 package (1 pound) round wonton or *gyoza* wrappers

2 egg whites, lightly beaten

Whenever I see dumplings on a menu, I always order them. Here I have filled them with a delicate blend of Chinese and New Mexican ingredients. The dumplings can be made, tray-frozen, and then bagged and stored in the freezer for several weeks. There is no need to thaw them before cooking.

In a skillet over medium heat, melt the butter. Add the shrimp and sauté until they turn pink, about 5 minutes. Remove from heat and cool to room temperature.

In a medium-sized bowl, combine the shrimp, ginger, spinach, egg, sesame oil, cornstarch mixture, cayenne, cilantro, and salt. Mix well and reserve.

In a small bowl, combine the tamari, chile oil, and serrano chiles; reserve.

Place 4 wonton wrappers on a flat surface. With a fingertip, lightly moisten the edge of each wrapper with egg white. Place a small mound of filling in the center of each round. Fold the wrapper over to form a half-moon shape and press firmly to seal. Repeat until all filling is used. As dumplings are formed, place them on a lightly floured baking sheet. Crimp edges along the round edge of the half-moon to form a decorative border. Preheat the oven to 200°F.

Bring a large pot filled with water to a boil. Gently drop about 15 of the dumplings into the water. Return to a gentle boil. Reduce heat to medium and simmer until dumplings float and wrappers are tender, 3 to 5 minutes. Remove with a slotted spoon to a heated platter and keep warm in the oven until all the dumplings are cooked.

Serve dumplings with the reserved tamari mixture as a dipping sauce.

MAKES *about 40 dumplings; serves 10.*

NOTE: *Asian chile oil is peanut or other vegetable oil that has been heated with dried hot red chiles and then strained. It is available in bottles in Asian markets.*

1 pound fresh mozzarella

1 pound cherry or currant tomatoes

12 fresh shiitake mushrooms

½ teaspoon chopped garlic

3 tablespoons pure olive oil

2 tablespoons dry sherry

¼ teaspoon salt

¼ teaspoon freshly ground black pepper

12 fresh basil leaves

¼ cup extra-virgin olive oil, for topping

1 teaspoon hot-pepper flakes, for garnish

During the days I lived in New York City's Soho, there was a little Italian place in the neighborhood called Joe's Dairy. Every afternoon by two o'clock, Joe's had made a batch of fresh mozzarella and I could never resist buying some. The cheese is delicious by itself or with any of dozens of different combinations of ingredients. This exquisite dish partners the fresh mozzarella with shiitake mushrooms, olive oil, and basil.

Preheat the oven to 450°F. Cut the mozzarella into slices about ¼ inch thick, forming 12 slices in all; reserve. Halve the cherry tomatoes; reserve. Remove and discard stems from mushrooms; place caps in a medium-sized bowl. Add the garlic, pure olive oil, sherry, salt, and pepper. Toss gently to coat mushrooms evenly.

Arrange mushrooms, cap side up, in a shallow baking pan or baking sheet and cover with foil. Bake for 7 minutes. Remove foil and bake for an additional 4 minutes. Let cool to room temperature.

On individual serving plates, form a line by alternating a basil leaf, mozzarella slice, and mushroom cap; repeat line 3 times on each plate. Place cherry tomatoes randomly around the edges. Drizzle with extra-virgin olive oil and sprinkle with pepper flakes.

SERVES 4.

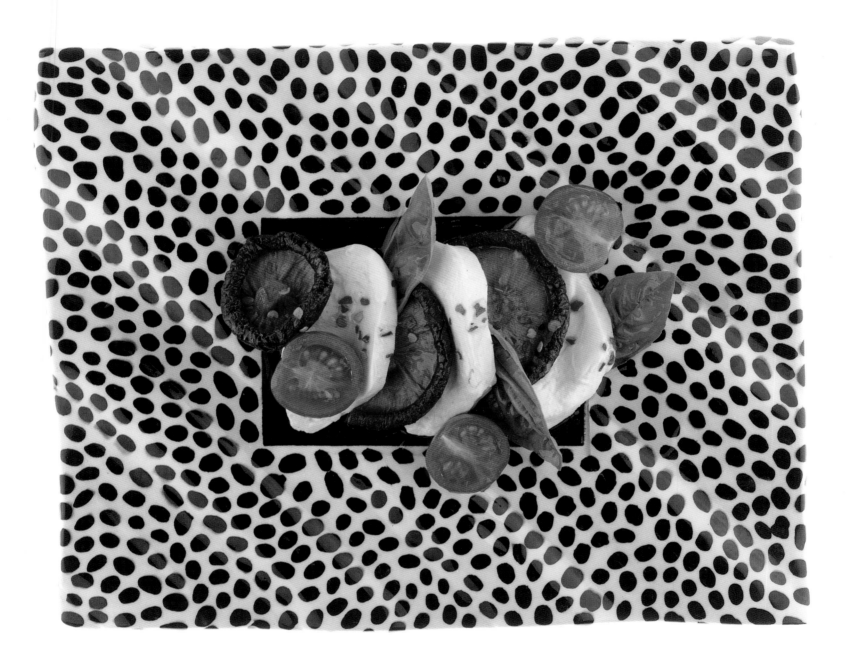

24 bluepoint oysters in the shell

1 small fresh Anaheim chile, seeded, deribbed, and
  finely minced

1 small red onion, finely minced

4 green onions, finely minced

1 medium-sized red bell pepper, seeded, deribbed,
  and finely minced

1 medium-sized yellow bell pepper, seeded,
  deribbed, and finely minced

1 tablespoon finely minced *gari*

1 tablespoon finely minced fresh cilantro

Juice of 1 lemon

¼ teaspoon salt

¼ teaspoon freshly ground black pepper

2 cups rock salt

4 to 8 small sprigs piñon or other pine, for garnish

1 lemon, quartered, for garnish

*To my mind, very few foods can compare with the extraordinary taste
of fresh raw oysters. No matter where you are, you feel as if you are
by the sea. The peppery sweet taste of pickled ginger subtly enhances
the delicate flavor of the oysters.*

*Wash the oysters under cold, running water (you may need a stiff brush
to remove any grit). Using an oyster knife, open each oyster, sliding
knife along upper and under sides of meat to sever muscles. Discard top
shells. Refrigerate oysters on the half shell until ready to serve.*

*In a medium-sized steel bowl, combine the chile, red onion, green
onion, red bell pepper, yellow bell pepper, gari, and cilantro; toss
lightly. Add lemon juice, salt, and black pepper; stir well.*

*Line individual serving dishes with the rock salt. Garnish with 1 or 2
sprigs of piñon. Place 6 oysters on each plate and top each with a spoonful
of the bell pepper mixture. Garnish with lemon wedges.*

SERVES *4.*

4 tablespoons unsalted butter

I tablespoon chopped garlic

1½ cups chopped leeks (white part only)

2 fresh serrano chiles, seeded, deribbed, and finely
chopped

2 fresh Anaheim chiles, seeded, deribbed, and finely
chopped

2 dried Chinese chiles, seeded and finely chopped

2 bay leaves

I tablespoon chopped fresh thyme

3 medium-sized potatoes, peeled and cut into
¼-inch dice

6 cups chicken stock

4 cups (I quart) heavy cream

1½ teaspoons kosher salt

I teaspoon freshly ground black pepper

½ teaspoon hot-pepper flakes

2 tablespoons balsamic vinegar

10 sprigs cilantro, for garnish

CHIMAYO CRÈME FRAÎCHE TOPPING

I teaspoon ground dried Chimayo chile

I teaspoon tomato paste

6 dashes Tabasco sauce

2 tablespoons mayonnaise

I cup crème fraîche

½ teaspoon salt

½ teaspoon white pepper

In this soup, a mild potato taste is combined with fiery chiles in a pleasing blend of cool flavors and warm spiciness. Serve chilled in hot weather or hot in wintry weather.

In a large saucepan over medium heat, melt the butter. Add the garlic, leeks, serrano and Anaheim chiles, dried chiles, bay leaves, and thyme. Sauté until leeks are translucent, about 5 minutes.

Add the potatoes and 2 cups of the stock. Cover, bring to a boil, reduce heat, and simmer 10 minutes. Add the remaining 4 cups stock and bring to a boil. Reduce heat and simmer, uncovered, until potato cubes fall apart when pierced with a fork, about 15 minutes.

Stir in the cream, salt, black pepper, and pepper flakes; simmer, uncovered, for 10 minutes. Transfer to a food processor or blender (in batches, if necessary) and purée until smooth. Return to saucepan and reheat. Add the vinegar; taste and adjust seasonings. Remove from heat, cool to room temperature, cover, and chill.

Just before serving the soup, make the crème fraîche topping. In a medium-sized bowl, combine the chile, tomato paste, and Tabasco; mix well. Fold in mayonnaise and crème fraîche, then add salt and pepper. Transfer to a squeeze bottle.

Ladle chilled soup into a tureen or large bowl. Squeeze a zigzag of the crème fraîche topping on the surface. Garnish with cilantro.

SERVES *10.*

3½ cups all-purpose flour

1½ tablespoons sugar

1 package active dry yeast

1½ teaspoons salt

½ teaspoon ground dried red chile

½ teaspoon freshly ground black pepper

1 tablespoon lukewarm water (105° to 115° F)

2 tablespoons milk

⅓ cup minced, roasted, and peeled fresh poblano chile at room temperature

¼ cup ground, minced, roasted, and peeled red bell pepper at room temperature

5 eggs at room temperature

9 ounces (½ pound plus 2 tablespoons) unsalted butter, cut into small pieces and softened

This recipe came into being by accident. When Santacafé first opened, a fellow chef and I tried to come up with a simple but impressive bread. She thought of a brioche and I suggested adding red and green chiles to it. The result was this recipe, which has been requested by more customers than any other item on our menu.

In the bowl of an electric mixer with a paddle attachment, combine the flour, sugar, yeast, salt, ground chile, and black pepper. Mix briefly on low speed. Increase speed to medium and add the water, milk, poblano chile, and bell pepper; beat well. Add the eggs, one at a time, mixing well after each addition. Change to the dough hook, and knead for 3 minutes. The dough will be very sticky. Add the butter to the dough, 1 piece at a time, and continue to knead until dough is smooth and shiny and the butter is completely incorporated, 10 to 20 minutes.

Transfer the dough to a lightly buttered bowl and flip the dough to coat it evenly with butter. Cover bowl with plastic wrap and allow dough to rise in a warm place until it has doubled in bulk, about 3 hours. Punch down the dough and turn it out onto a lightly floured surface. With heavily floured hands, knead for 5 minutes. Return to a buttered bowl and flip dough to coat evenly; cover and chill dough for at least 6 hours or overnight in the refrigerator.

Remove the dough from the refrigerator and shape the cold dough into 2 small loaves. Place in 2 buttered 4- by 9-inch loaf pans, cover with a tea towel, and let rise in a warm place until the dough fills the loaf pans and does not spring back when gently pressed, about 1 hour.

Preheat the oven to 375°F. Bake the loaves in the middle of the oven until they are golden and sound hollow when tapped, about 30 minutes. Remove loaves from oven and turn them out onto wire racks to cool.

MAKES *2 loaves.*

1 red bell pepper, seeded, deribbed, and cut into
  $\frac{1}{4}$-inch-wide strips
2 boneless roasted pheasant or duck breasts
  (4 ounces each), cut into $\frac{1}{4}$-inch-wide strips
1 small carrot, finely julienned
$\frac{1}{2}$ cup julienned napa cabbage
$\frac{1}{4}$ cup julienned spinach
3 cloves garlic, finely chopped
1 stalk celery, finely julienned
1 tablespoon chopped fresh cilantro
$\frac{1}{4}$ cup chopped red onion
Salt and freshly ground black pepper to taste
1 package (1 pound) rice paper wrappers (see Note)
4 egg whites, lightly beaten
Peanut oil for deep-frying
1 head red leaf or butter lettuce
$\frac{1}{2}$ pound linguine, cooked, drained, and cooled
1 bunch fresh mint

3-CHILE DIPPING SAUCE
6 cloves garlic
$\frac{1}{4}$ cup sugar
3 fresh Thai chiles, seeded and deribbed
2 fresh serrano chiles, seeded and deribbed
$\frac{1}{2}$ dried Chinese chile, seeded
2 limes, juiced with pulp
$\frac{1}{2}$ cup Vietnamese fish sauce
1 cup water
1 teaspoon distilled white vinegar
Thin carrot strips, for garnish

I wanted to come up with a new kind of Vietnamese spring roll—to create a variation that would make the wonderfully crisp roll very special. What I settled on was a filling of pheasant and napa cabbage and a sauce that uses three different chile varieties. These rolls, which are very popular at Santacafé, are ideal hors d'oeuvres.

In a large bowl, gently toss together the bell pepper, pheasant, carrot, cabbage, spinach, garlic, celery, cilantro, and onion. Season with salt and pepper.

Place a rice paper round on a dry flat surface (such as a Formica countertop). Brush the surface of the wrapper with egg white. Let stand a few seconds to soften. Place a heaping spoonful of filling about one fourth of the way in from the top edge of the wrapper. Spread filling into a rectangular shape, about ¾ inch wide and 5 inches long. Fold over top of the wrapper to cover filling, then roll up, folding in sides after second turn. The finished spring roll should resemble a thin egg roll. Repeat until all the filling is used.

To make the sauce, combine the garlic, sugar, chiles, and lime juice in a food processor or blender. Process until minced. Add fish sauce, water, and vinegar and mix well. Set aside.

To cook the spring rolls, pour the oil into a large saucepan to a depth of at least 4 inches. Heat oil to 375°F. Drop spring rolls into oil, a few at a time, and fry until golden brown, about 4 minutes; do not crowd the pan. Remove with a slotted utensil to paper towels to drain briefly. Cut each roll into 3 pieces.

To serve, divide sauce among individual bowls or place in a large bowl. Garnish with carrot strips. The spring rolls may be eaten plain or they may be wrapped inside a lettuce leaf with a small amount of pasta and a few mint leaves. In either case, dip them into the sauce and enjoy!

SERVES *8 to 10.*

NOTE: *Rice paper rounds, usually measuring from 6 to 8 inches, are sold in 1-pound packages in shops carrying Southeast Asian foods. You will need only a partial package to make these rolls. Wrap the remaining rounds tightly and store at room temperature.*

TO CONTINUE

BEET PASTA DOUGH

2 cups all-purpose flour

3 cups semolina flour, or as needed

¼ teaspoon salt

4 eggs

½ cup puréed, cooked beet (I medium beet)

2 tablespoons olive oil

CHEESE FILLING

I cup ricotta cheese

½ cup finely shredded mozzarella

½ cup freshly grated Parmesan cheese

2 tablespoons crumbled goat cheese

2 eggs

I medium-sized carrot, peeled and coarsely grated
   or finely chopped

¼ cup well-drained, chopped, cooked spinach
   (about ¼ pound uncooked)

2 tablespoons chopped fresh parsley

Pinch freshly grated nutmeg

½ teaspoon kosher salt

½ teaspoon freshly ground black pepper

½ cup extra-virgin olive oil, for serving

40 fresh leaves purple basil, for serving

The delicate pink of beet raviolis accented by deep burgundy basil leaves makes for a simple but striking presentation.

To make the pasta dough, combine the flours and salt in a food processor. With the machine running, gradually add the eggs and beet purée through the feed tube. Then slowly add the oil and continue to process until mixture forms a mass that holds together. Remove dough from processor bowl and knead on a lightly floured board until smooth, at least 5 minutes. Dough should be firm and not sticky. Add more semolina if necessary to achieve proper consistency. Form into a smooth ball, cover with plastic wrap, and refrigerate for at least 2 hours.

To make the filling, combine the 4 cheeses in a medium bowl and stir to mix with a wooden spoon. Stir in the remaining ingredients, blending thoroughly. Cover and refrigerate until you are ready to form the raviolis.

To roll out the dough on a pasta machine, follow the manufacturer's instructions. Work with only a small portion of dough at a time, keeping remaining dough covered. Put the dough through the rollers several times until the sheet is as thin as a knife blade. Dust the sheet with flour if dough starts to become too sticky. Repeat with the remaining dough. Cut the sheets into an even number of 10-inch-long pieces and transfer pieces to a flour-dusted surface.

To form the raviolis, place small mounds of the cheese filling on one of the dough sheets, arranging them evenly and allowing enough space between them for cutting. With a soft-bristled brush, lightly paint lines of water between the mounds. Place a second sheet on top of the first and, with your fingertips, press pasta sheets together between the mounds. With a pastry wheel or sharp knife, cut out raviolis. If necessary, again press together edges of raviolis to ensure they are well sealed. Place raviolis on a lightly floured surface. Repeat with the remaining dough sheets and filling.

Preheat the oven to 200°F. Bring a large pot filled with salted water to a boil. Add raviolis, a few at a time, to boiling water; do not crowd the raviolis in the pot. Return to a gentle boil. Reduce heat to medium and simmer until raviolis float and are cooked through, about 5 minutes. Remove with a slotted utensil to a heated platter and keep warm in the oven until all the raviolis are cooked.

To serve the raviolis, drizzle with the olive oil and garnish with basil.

SERVES *6 to 8.*

4 whole chicken breasts (about 12 ounces each),
    boned and skinned

Juice of 2 oranges

Juice of 2 limes

Juice of 1 lemon

¼ cup olive oil

1½ teaspoons ground Sichuan peppercorns

½ teaspoon freshly ground black pepper

4 cloves garlic, chopped

1½ teaspoons grated fresh ginger

4 shallots, chopped

1 tablespoon chopped fresh cilantro

1 teaspoon kosher salt

¼ cup bottled teriyaki sauce

½ teaspoon cumin seed, lightly toasted in a dry pan

Dash hot-pepper flakes

1 fresh poblano chile, seeded, deribbed, and sliced
    into ¼-inch-wide rings

1 fresh Anaheim chile, seeded, deribbed, and sliced
    into ¼-inch-wide rings

3 fresh serrano chiles, seeded and deribbed, if
    desired, and finely minced

1 red bell pepper, seeded, deribbed, and cut
    lengthwise into ¼-inch-wide strips

1 yellow bell pepper, seeded, deribbed, and cut
    lengthwise into ¼-inch-wide strips

1 large carrot, peeled and cut into matchstick pieces

1 large red onion, thinly sliced lengthwise

4 large flour tortillas

1 Maui or other sweet onion, thinly sliced crosswise,
    for garnish

Fajitas are very popular these days, and with the addition of a few Asian ingredients, they become even more irresistible. Shrimp, scallops, beef, or pork can be substituted for the chicken in this recipe with equally delicious results.

Slice the chicken meat into ½-inch-wide strips; reserve.

In a large bowl, combine the orange, lime, and lemon juices, oil, Sichuan and black peppers, garlic, ginger, shallots, cilantro, salt, teriyaki sauce, cumin seed, and pepper flakes. Whisk to combine. Add chicken to bowl, mix well, cover, and refrigerate for 1½ hours. Add all the fresh chiles, bell peppers, carrot, and red onion and toss to mix. Re-cover and refrigerate for 30 minutes.

Heat a wok or large, heavy-bottomed skillet over high heat. When the pan is very hot, scoop up the chicken and vegetables with a slotted utensil, draining well, and add to the pan. Sauté until chicken is cooked through, about 3 to 5 minutes. Taste and correct seasonings. Cover and keep warm on the stove top.

Meanwhile, steam the tortillas, or lightly grill them over hot coals. Place 1 tortilla on each plate and top with one fourth of the chicken-vegetable mixture. Garnish with Maui onion.

SERVES *4.*

1 cup olive oil

2 cloves garlic, chopped

1 teaspoon hot-pepper flakes

$\frac{1}{4}$ cup seasoned rice vinegar

2 ears of corn, husks turned down to expose whole ear

1 carrot, peeled and quartered lengthwise

1 yellow summer squash, trimmed and halved
   lengthwise

1 red onion, quartered lengthwise

1 head garlic, halved crosswise

1 Japanese eggplant, trimmed and quartered
   lengthwise

1 acorn squash, halved crosswise, peeled, seeded,
   and cut into $\frac{1}{2}$-inch-wide slices

6 green onions, trimmed

2 fresh Anaheim chiles

SESAME-SAGE SAUCE

1 cup homemade mayonnaise

$1\frac{1}{2}$ tablespoons seasoned rice vinegar

1 tablespoon tamari or soy sauce

Juice of $\frac{1}{2}$ lemon

$2\frac{1}{2}$ tablespoons white sesame seed, toasted

1 fresh Anaheim chile, chopped

2 cloves garlic, minced

$1\frac{1}{2}$ tablespoons Dijon-style mustard

1 teaspoon finely chopped fresh sage

Black sesame seed, for garnish

Sage grows like crazy in New Mexico and I have truly come to love cooking with it. Lightly grilled vegetables dipped in a rich sage sauce make a perfect light autumn dinner.

In a large bowl, whisk together the oil, garlic, pepper flakes, and vinegar. Add the corn, carrot, summer squash, red onion, garlic, eggplant, acorn squash, green onions, and chiles. Toss gently. Marinate at room temperature for 1 hour.

To make the sage sauce, spoon the mayonnaise into a glass bowl. Stir in vinegar, tamari, lemon juice, white sesame seed, chile, garlic, mustard, and sage. Garnish with black sesame seed. Cover and chill.

Prepare a fire in a charcoal grill. Remove vegetables from marinade and arrange them on the grill over medium-hot coals. Cook until tender, about 4 minutes on each side. Serve sauce on the side.

SERVES *4.*

1 cup all-purpose flour

3 cups fine semolina flour, or as needed

¾ teaspoon salt

6 eggs

6 tablespoons olive oil

1 teaspoon chopped garlic

1 pound sea scallops, halved

¼ teaspoon freshly ground black pepper

Salt, to taste, for cooking pasta

Toasted sesame seed, for garnish

Fresh serrano chiles, thinly sliced, for garnish

SPICY BROWN SAUCE

1¾ cups stock

1½ teaspoons chopped fresh ginger

5 cloves garlic, chopped

3 shallots, chopped

5 green onions, including 2 inches of green tops
chopped

4 fresh serrano chiles, seeded, if desired, and chopped

1 dried Chinese chile, chopped

¼ cup soy sauce

¼ cup bottled teriyaki sauce

2 tablespoons brown sugar

Juice of 1 orange

6 tablespoons water

3 dashes Tabasco sauce

1 tablespoon Chinese black vinegar

1 teaspoon cornstarch, dissolved in 1 tablespoon water

The delicate pasta folds that envelop tender sea scallops recall ribbons of seaweed gently rolling in the ocean depths.

To make the pasta dough, combine the flours and ½ teaspoon of the salt in a food processor. With the machine running, gradually add the eggs through the feed tube. Then slowly add 3 tablespoons of the oil and continue to process until mixture forms a mass that holds together. Remove dough from processor bowl and knead on a lightly floured board until smooth, at least 5 minutes. Dough should be firm and not sticky. Add more semolina if necessary to achieve proper consistency. Form into a smooth ball, cover with plastic wrap, and refrigerate for at least 2 hours.

To roll out the dough on a pasta machine, follow the manufacturer's instructions. Work with only a small portion of dough at a time, keeping remaining dough covered. Put the dough through the rollers several times until the sheet is as thin as a knife blade. Dust the sheet with flour if dough starts to become too sticky. Cut sheet into 8-inch squares and repeat with the remaining dough. As the squares are cut, transfer them to a flour-dusted tea towel. You should have 6 to 8 squares in all.

To make the sauce, in a saucepan combine the stock, ginger, garlic, shallots, green onions, and serrano and Chinese chiles. Simmer over medium heat for 5 to 7 minutes. Add all the remaining ingredients except cornstarch mixture. Bring to a boil and whisk in cornstarch mixture. Cook, stirring, until sauce is thick enough to coat a spoon, about 7 to 10 minutes. Taste and correct seasonings. Keep warm.

Bring a large pot filled with water to a boil. Meanwhile, place a large heavy-bottomed sauté pan over medium-high heat. Add the remaining 3 tablespoons oil to the pan. When oil is hot, add the garlic and scallops and sauté for 2 minutes. Add the remaining ¼ teaspoon salt and pepper and sauté until scallops are cooked through, about 4 minutes; be careful not to overcook.

While the scallops are cooking, salt the boiling water. When water returns to a boil, add pasta and cook until just done, about 4 minutes. Arrange 1 noodle ribbon across each individual serving plate. Ladle sparingly with sauce and top with scallops. Garnish with sesame seed and serrano chile.

SERVES *6 to 8.*

4 cloves garlic, chopped

1 teaspoon chopped fresh rosemary

¼ cup olive oil

½ cup bottled pomegranate juice

½ teaspoon kosher salt

½ teaspoon freshly ground black pepper

12 loin lamb chops, about 1¼ inches thick and
    french-cut

Fresh mint sprigs, for garnish

APPLE-MINT CHUTNEY

10 Granny Smith apples, cored, peeled, and coarsely
    chopped

2 fresh jalapeño chiles, seeded and finely chopped

1 large white onion, finely chopped

¼ cup dried currants

¼ cup pure maple syrup

¼ cup firmly packed brown sugar

1 teaspoon ground cinnamon

½ teaspoon freshly grated nutmeg

4 cloves garlic

1 tablespoon chopped fresh mint

⅓ cup apple cider vinegar

¼ teaspoon kosher salt

½ teaspoon freshly ground black pepper

GREEN CHILE COUNTRY-STYLE POTATOES

3 carrots, peeled and quartered crosswise

5 medium-sized russet potatoes, quartered

⅓ cup sour cream

4 tablespoons unsalted butter, softened

5 dashes Tabasco sauce

¼ cup chopped green onion, including 2 inches of
    green tops

½ cup chopped fresh green chile

Pinch cayenne pepper

1 teaspoon kosher salt

½ teaspoon freshly ground black pepper

A northern California friend first told me about marinating lamb in pomegranate juice, and it continues to be my favorite way to prepare it. At Santacafé the chile-laced mashed potatoes are in as much demand as the lamb chops. Look for the pomegranate juice in Middle Eastern grocery stores and gourmet-foods shops.

In a medium-sized bowl, combine the garlic, rosemary, oil, pomegranate juice, salt, and pepper. Mix well. In a shallow, nonmetallic container, arrange the lamb chops. Pour pomegranate mixture over lamb and turn chops to coat evenly. Let stand for 3 hours at room temperature.

To make the chutney, combine all the ingredients in a large, heavy-bottomed pot over high heat. Bring to a boil, reduce the heat to medium, and simmer, uncovered, until apples are tender, about 30 minutes. Let cool, cover, and refrigerate until ready to use.

To make the mashed potatoes, combine the carrots, potatoes, and water to cover in a large pot. Bring to a boil over high heat and cook until vegetables are tender, about 30 minutes; test with a fork. While potatoes and carrots are cooking, prepare a fire in a charcoal grill.

Preheat the oven to 200°F. Drain carrots and potatoes and coarsely mash with a hand masher or in an electric mixer with a paddle attachment. Add all the remaining mashed potato ingredients and continue to mash until desired smoothness is achieved. Taste and correct seasonings; cover and keep warm in the oven.

Remove lamb chops from marinade and place on grill over hot coals. Grill until done as desired, about 4 minutes per side for medium-rare. Arrange on a heated plate with a small dish of chutney on the side. Garnish with mint. Serve with mashed potatoes.

SERVES *4.*

3 tablespoons unsalted butter

½ cup sliced fresh oyster mushrooms (see Note)

½ cup sliced fresh shiitake mushrooms

½ cup finely minced red onion

½ cup finely minced fresh Anaheim chile

1½ tablespoons chopped garlic

2 eggs

½ cup ricotta cheese

½ cup freshly shredded mozzarella cheese

2 teaspoons kosher salt

1 teaspoon freshly ground black pepper

1 tablespoon finely chopped fresh basil

1 teaspoon chopped fresh thyme leaves

1 teaspoon chopped fresh rosemary

1 tablespoon chopped fresh flat-leaf parsley

1 teaspoon dried oregano

2 tablespoons peanut oil

12 corn tortillas

1 cup freshly shredded Sonoma pepper jack cheese

12 sprigs fresh cilantro, for garnish

ROASTED RED PEPPER SAUCE

3 red bell peppers, roasted, peeled, and seeded

1 teaspoon minced garlic

1 tablespoon balsamic vinegar

1 teaspoon grated fresh ginger

1 teaspoon salt

Pinch cayenne pepper

5 dashes Tabasco sauce

3 tablespoons tomato sauce

¼ teaspoon white pepper

3 tablespoons olive oil

On a trip to Puerto Vallarta I found a marvelous place that served great spinach enchiladas. When I returned home I decided to create an enchilada with a Far Eastern accent. The result is a rich mushroom and cheese filling complemented by a ginger-spiked sauce.

Place a 12-inch skillet over medium-high heat. When the skillet is hot, add 2 tablespoons of the butter and tip the pan to coat bottom evenly. Add the oyster and shiitake mushrooms, red onion, Anaheim chile, and garlic; sauté for 5 minutes. Remove pan from heat and transfer sautéed mixture to a large bowl; let cool to room temperature. Stir in eggs, ricotta, mozzarella, salt, pepper, basil, thyme, rosemary, parsley, and oregano. Taste and correct seasonings.

Preheat the oven to 400°F. Place a heavy-bottomed skillet over medium heat and add the oil. When the oil is hot, grasp a tortilla with a pair of tongs and slip the tortilla into the hot oil. After 30 seconds, flip the tortilla and allow to cook for another 30 seconds. Remove the tortillas to plates lined with paper towels to absorb the oil.

Generously butter a large baking dish with the remaining 1 tablespoon butter. Place about 3 tablespoons of the cheese-mushroom mixture in the center and about one third in from the edge of a tortilla. Gently roll into a compact cylinder. Repeat with remaining tortillas and filling, arranging them, seam side down, in a single layer in the dish. Cover with aluminum foil and bake until piping hot, about 15 minutes.

Meanwhile, make the sauce. Combine all the ingredients in a food processor or blender. Process until smooth, about 5 minutes. Transfer the sauce to a saucepan and place over medium heat until hot. Keep warm.

Preheat the broiler for 5 minutes. Place a ladleful of sauce onto each of 4 heated flameproof dinner plates. Place 3 hot enchiladas atop the sauce in the center of each plate and sprinkle with jack cheese; slip each plate under the preheated broiler until the cheese melts, about 2 minutes. Garnish each serving with 3 cilantro sprigs.

SERVES *4.*

NOTE: *Oyster mushrooms have caps shaped like fans and range in color from white to tan. They taste best when young, about 1 to 2 inches in diameter. Some people feel that the mild flavor of the oyster mushroom is reminiscent of its bivalve namesake.*

3 cups small Boston lettuce leaves

I head radicchio

2 whole smoked pheasant breasts, boned and
    thinly sliced

2 ripe pears, halved lengthwise, cored, and thinly
    sliced lengthwise

$\frac{1}{4}$ cup pine nuts, lightly toasted

Pesticide-free nasturtium flowers, for garnish

VINAIGRETTE

$2\frac{1}{2}$ tablespoons red wine vinegar

Juice of $\frac{1}{2}$ large lemon

$1\frac{1}{2}$ tablespoons sugar

$\frac{3}{4}$ cup olive oil

I teaspoon finely minced seeded fresh serrano chile

2 teaspoons finely chopped cilantro

$\frac{1}{2}$ teaspoon salt

$\frac{1}{2}$ teaspoon freshly ground black pepper

I prefer to use smoked pheasant breasts for this salad, but smoked chicken or duck breasts may be substituted if pheasant is unavailable. The salad can open a meal or it can be served as a light main course.

To make the vinaigrette, combine the vinegar, lemon juice, and sugar in a bowl; whisk to blend. Slowly whisk in the oil, then stir in the chile, cilantro, salt, and pepper. Set aside.

    If the lettuce leaves are small, use them whole. If the leaves are large, cut them into ½-inch-wide strips. Cut the radicchio into fine julienne strips.

    Place one fourth of the lettuce in a nest on one half of each of 4 individual serving plates. Sprinkle one fourth of the radicchio over each lettuce nest. On the other half of each plate, arrange the slices from a pheasant breast half, alternating them with slices from a pear half.

    Just before serving, lightly dress each salad with vinaigrette. Garnish with pine nuts and nasturtium flowers.

SERVES 4.

BLACK AND YELLOW PASTA DOUGHS

2 cups semolina flour

1 cup all-purpose flour

2 teaspoons salt

1 teaspoon squid or cuttlefish ink, mixed with
   3 tablespoons water

4 eggs

About 3 tablespoons olive oil

15 threads saffron, mixed with 3 tablespoons water

GINGER SHRIMP

2 pounds large shrimp, peeled and deveined

2 teaspoons grated fresh ginger

¼ cup pure olive oil

2 tablespoons unsalted butter

4 leeks, trimmed and cut into ¼- by 1-inch pieces

3 red bell peppers, seeded, deribbed, and cut into
   ¼-inch squares

4 fresh serrano chiles, seeded, deribbed, and finely
   chopped

6 cloves garlic, chopped

¼ cup chopped mixed fresh herbs such as parsley,
   basil, tarragon, cilantro, and thyme, in any
   combination

½ cup extra-virgin olive oil

1 teaspoon kosher salt

1½ teaspoons freshly ground black pepper

In this stunning dish, black and yellow pastas are partnered with plump, lightly sautéed shrimp. The shellfish are subtly seasoned to enhance and not obscure the wonderful taste of the fresh fettuccine. You will need about two pounds of pasta for this dish. If you do not wish to make your own, fresh fettuccine in a variety of flavors is available in most specialty-foods shops.

To make the black pasta dough, combine 1 cup of the semolina flour, ½ cup of the all-purpose flour, and 1 teaspoon of the salt in a food processor. With the machine running, gradually add the diluted squid ink and 2 of the eggs through the feed tube. Then slowly add only enough olive oil for the mixture to form a mass that holds together; you will need about 1½ tablespoons.

Turn dough out onto a lightly floured board and knead until smooth, at least 5 minutes. Dough should be firm and not sticky. Form into a smooth ball, cover with plastic wrap, and refrigerate for 2 hours.

Make the yellow pasta according to these same directions, substituting the saffron-water mixture for diluted squid ink. Form into a smooth ball, cover with plastic wrap, and refrigerate for 2 hours.

To begin preparing the shrimp, combine the shrimp, ginger, and pure olive oil in a medium bowl. Cover and marinate for 1 hour.

To roll out the dough on a pasta machine, follow the manufacturer's instructions. Work with only a small portion of dough at a time and keep the remaining dough covered. Put the dough through the rollers several times until the sheet is as thin as a knife blade. Dust the sheet with flour if dough starts to become too sticky. Adjust the blades for fettuccine and pass the sheet through the cutters. Hang the noodles on a rack or lay them out on a flour-dusted towel. Repeat with the remaining dough.

To continue preparing the shrimp, heat a 12-inch skillet over high heat until very hot. Add the butter. When the butter melts, add the leeks, bell peppers, chiles, and garlic. Sauté until soft, about 5 minutes. Add the shrimp-oil mixture and sauté shrimp until they just turn pink and curl, about 5 minutes. Stir in herbs.

Meanwhile, bring a large pot filled with salted water to a boil. Add the black and yellow pasta and cook until just done, about 3 minutes. Drain pasta and place in a large heated serving dish. Add shrimp mixture, extra-virgin olive oil, salt, and pepper. Toss and serve immediately.

SERVES *6.*

$3\frac{1}{3}$ cups short-grain white rice

4 cups cold water

6 tablespoons seasoned rice vinegar

8 sheets *nori*, toasted and cut in half

1 tablespoon ground dried red chile

$\frac{1}{2}$ cup prepared *wasabi*

2 smoked trout (8 ounces each), deboned and cut
   crosswise into $\frac{1}{4}$-inch pieces

8 green onions, including 2 inches of green tops
   halved lengthwise

1 carrot, peeled, blanched, and cut into $\frac{1}{8}$-inch-square
   matchstick pieces

8 green beans, blanched

1 pound fresh lean tuna fillet, sliced across the grain
   into $\frac{1}{4}$-inch-thick pieces, then cut crosswise into
   thirds

1 large red bell pepper, roasted, peeled, seeded,
   deribbed and julienned

1 cup *gari*, for serving

$\frac{1}{2}$ cup tamari, for serving

Maki rolls in Japan are like raviolis in Italy. They come filled with just about anything from tuna to pineapple. Here I have created two different fillings, one with smoked trout and one with tuna. Look for the bamboo sushi rolling mat in a store that specializes in Japanese cooking utensils.

In a heavy-bottomed, medium-sized pot, combine the rice and water. Cover, place over medium heat, and bring to a boil. Raise heat to high and boil for 2 minutes. Reduce heat to medium and cook for 5 minutes. Reduce heat to low and cook for 15 minutes or until all water has been absorbed. Turn heat off and let rice stand, covered, for an additional 13 minutes. Do not uncover pot even to peek. To prepare rice in an electric rice cooker, follow manufacturer's instructions.

Using a rice paddle or flat wooden spoon, spread the hot rice in a thin layer in a shallow wooden or plastic vessel. Lightly sprinkle with the rice vinegar and gently turn the rice with horizontal cutting strokes. At the same time, cool the rice quickly and thoroughly to room temperature with a hand fan or an electric fan. When cool, cover rice with a damp cloth. Do not refrigerate. Rice will keep for up to 7 hours at room temperature.

For the trout-filled rolls, cover a bamboo sushi mat completely with clear plastic wrap. Position the mat so it rolls away from you. Place half a sheet of nori *at end of mat closest to you. With dampened hands, spread a ¼-inch-thick layer of rice evenly over the* nori. *Dust rice evenly with a little of the chile. Flip the* nori *so that the rice side is against the plastic wrap. With your index finger, spread a small amount of* wasabi *in a line down the center of the* nori. *On top of this, place a line of smoked trout pieces. Then lay onion pieces, carrot pieces, and a green bean on top of trout. Working away from you, roll sushi up in mat and shape it by pressing roll firmly. Unroll mat and set roll aside. Repeat within remaining trout and vegetables. Reserve rolls.*

For the tuna-filled rolls, remove the plastic wrap from the sushi mat. Place half a sheet of nori *at end of mat closest to you. Spread a ¼-inch-thick layer of rice evenly over mat, leaving a ⅞-inch border uncovered along edge farthest from you. With your index finger, spread a small amount of* wasabi *in a line down the length of the center of the rice. On top of this place a line of tuna and then a line of roasted pepper strips. Working away from you, roll sushi up in mat and shape it by pressing roll firmly. Moisten the margin of* nori *and seal as tightly as possible. Unroll and set roll aside. Repeat with remaining tuna and pepper strips.*

To serve, cut each sushi roll into sixths. Serve with gari, tamari, *and the remaining* wasabi *on the side.*

SERVES *8.*

3 tablespoons unsalted butter

10 cloves garlic, finely chopped

1½ cups chopped red onion

2 bay leaves

2 tablespoons chopped fresh cilantro

2 teaspoons freshly ground, toasted cumin seed

2 teaspoons freshly ground coriander seed

1 teaspoon dried Mexican oregano leaves

¼ teaspoon ground dried Chimayo chile

2 pounds stew beef, cut into ½-inch cubes

3 tablespoons tomato paste

8 fresh serrano chiles

1 dried ancho chile, finely chopped

2 fresh Anaheim chiles, finely chopped

½ cup beef stock

¼ cup sherry

1 cup cooked black beans

1 cup cooked white beans

1 cup cooked pinto beans

1 tablespoon kosher salt

1 teaspoon freshly ground black pepper

½ pound white Cheddar cheese, shredded, for garnish

1 teaspoon crushed hot-pepper flakes, for garnish

20 sprigs cilantro, for garnish

8 to 10 green onions, trimmed and grilled, for garnish

8 to 10 red onion quarters, grilled, for garnish

Three varieties of fresh chiles and beans, traditional New Mexican ingredients, are combined to make a hearty, flavorful chili.

In a large 4- to 6-inch-deep skillet or saucepan over medium-high heat, melt the butter. Add the garlic, chopped onion, bay leaves, cilantro, cumin, coriander, oregano, and Chimayo chile and sauté until onion is translucent, about 5 minutes. Add the beef and tomato paste and sauté for 10 minutes. Finely chop 4 of the serrano chiles and add to the skillet with the ancho and Anaheim chiles. Sauté, stirring occasionally, for 5 minutes. Add the stock, sherry, all the beans, salt, and pepper. Reduce heat to low and simmer, uncovered, for 20 minutes. Taste and correct seasonings.

Thinly slice the remaining 4 serrano chiles. Ladle chili into individual serving bowls. Garnish with Cheddar, sliced serrano chiles, pepper flakes, and cilantro. Place 1 green onion on one side of each bowl and a red onion quarter on the other side.

SERVES *8 to 10.*

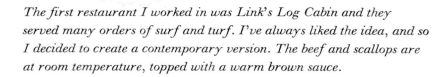

1 filet mignon (about 2 pounds), trimmed of excess fat

Olive oil, salt, and freshly ground black pepper, for rubbing on filet mignon

1 pound large sea scallops

2 tablespoons olive oil

Salt and freshly ground black pepper, to taste

1 pound artichoke spaghetti

½ cup Asian sesame oil

1 tablespoon sesame seed, toasted, for garnish

16 fresh whole chives, for garnish

EGGPLANT SALSA

3 Japanese eggplants, trimmed and cut into small pieces

1 red onion, coarsely chopped

6 green onions, including some green tops, chopped

1 red bell pepper, seeded, deribbed, and chopped

1 fresh Anaheim chile, seeded, deribbed, and cut into thin rings

4 cloves garlic, finely chopped

2 tablespoons Asian sesame oil

1 tablespoon brown sugar

½ teaspoon grated fresh ginger

2 tablespoons balsamic vinegar

1 tablespoon *gari*, finely chopped

1 tablespoon chopped fresh cilantro

BROWN SAUCE

1 tablespoon Asian sesame oil

1 teaspoon finely chopped fresh ginger

2 shallots, finely chopped

2 fresh serrano chiles, seeded, deribbed, and chopped

4 cloves garlic, finely chopped

1 cup water

1 cup chicken stock

¼ cup soy sauce

¼ cup bottled teriyaki sauce

1 tablespoon brown sugar

Juice of 1 orange

1 teaspoon cornstarch, dissolved in 2 tablespoons water

1 tablespoon Chinese black vinegar

The first restaurant I worked in was Link's Log Cabin and they served many orders of surf and turf. I've always liked the idea, and so I decided to create a contemporary version. The beef and scallops are at room temperature, topped with a warm brown sauce.

Preheat the broiler or prepare a fire in a charcoal grill. Rub the filet mignon well with oil, salt, and pepper. Broil or grill the filet, turning to cook it on each of its 4 sides, until medium-rare, 4 to 5 minutes per side. Set aside.

In a medium-sized bowl, toss together the scallops, olive oil, salt, and pepper. Broil or grill, turning once, until opaque, about 2 minutes per side. Set aside.

Meanwhile, fill a large pot with water and bring to a boil. Add salt and spaghetti and cook until al dente. Drain in a colander, rinse under cold water to cool, and drain again. Transfer to a bowl and toss with ¼ cup of the sesame oil. Divide spaghetti into 8 equal portions. Working quickly, tightly spiral each portion around a long cooking fork. Slide the spiral off the fork onto a flat plate or tray. Repeat with remaining pasta, cover, and set aside.

To make the salsa, preheat the oven to 375°F. In a large bowl, combine all the ingredients except gari and cilantro. Toss well and transfer to a shallow baking pan. Cover with aluminum foil and bake until eggplant is tender, about 20 minutes. Let cool to room temperature, then stir in gari and cilantro.

While the salsa is cooking, make the sauce. In a medium-sized saucepan over medium heat, warm the oil. Add the ginger, shallots, chiles, and garlic. Sauté until shallots and ginger are soft, about 5 minutes. Add all the remaining ingredients. Simmer, uncovered, stirring occasionally, until sauce is thick enough to coat the back of a wooden spoon, 15 to 20 minutes. Keep sauce warm.

To serve, thinly slice filet into ¼-inch-thick slices. Arrange several slices at one end of each of 8 oval plates. Place a spoonful of the salsa on top of the slices (reserve any leftover salsa for another use). In the middle of each plate position a spiral of spaghetti and drizzle with an equal amount of the remaining ¼ cup sesame oil (about 1½ teaspoons per serving). Sprinkle each spiral with sesame seed. At the other end of the plate place 2 or 3 scallops, depending upon their size. Ladle about 3 tablespoons of the warm sauce over the scallops. Garnish each serving with 2 chives crisscrossed on the center of the plate.

SERVES *8.*

PASTA DOUGH

2 cups fine semolina flour

1 cup all-purpose flour

4 teaspoons salt

5 eggs

2 tablespoons extra-virgin olive oil

Ice water, for cooling pasta

SHIITAKE FILLING

2 tablespoons extra-virgin olive oil

15 fresh shiitake mushrooms, stemmed and coarsely
   chopped

$\frac{1}{2}$ cup shredded fontina cheese

3 cups ricotta cheese

$\frac{1}{4}$ cup finely grated fresh Parmesan cheese

1 pound baked Virginia ham, thinly sliced and cut
   into $\frac{1}{2}$-inch squares

2 eggs

1 teaspoon hot-pepper flakes

$\frac{1}{2}$ teaspoon freshly ground black pepper

1 tablespoon finely chopped fresh cilantro

CREAM SAUCE

1 cup unsalted butter

2 cups heavy cream

$\frac{1}{4}$ cup tomato paste

$\frac{1}{2}$ teaspoon ground dried red chile

1 teaspoon kosher salt

1 teaspoon freshly ground black pepper

Melted unsalted butter, for brushing on pasta

Flat-leaf parsley sprigs, for garnish

I first tasted pasta roses in Ravello, overlooking Italy's Amalfi coast. They have become a favorite, lending themselves to countless fillings.

To make the pasta dough, combine the flours and 2 teaspoons of the salt in a food processor. With the machine running, gradually add the eggs and oil through the feed tube. Process until mixture forms a mass that holds together, about 2 minutes. Remove dough from processor and knead on a lightly floured board until smooth, about 2 minutes. Form into a smooth ball, cover with plastic wrap, and refrigerate for 4 hours.

To roll out the dough on a pasta machine, follow the manufacturer's instructions. Work with only a small portion of dough at a time, keeping remaining dough covered. Put the dough through the rollers several times until the sheet is as thin as a knife blade. Dust the sheet with flour if dough starts to become too sticky. Trim each sheet into straight-sided strips about 10 inches long and 6 inches wide. Repeat with remaining dough. As the strips are cut, transfer them to a flour-dusted tea towel.

Bring a large pot filled with water to a boil and add the remaining 2 teaspoons salt. When the water returns to a boil, drop in 3 pasta strips. Cook for 45 seconds, then retrieve with a slotted utensil, plunge into ice water, and remove to a tea towel. Repeat with remaining strips.

To make the filling, place a sauté pan over high heat and add the oil. Add the mushrooms, reduce heat to medium, and sauté for 5 minutes. Remove from heat and let cool. In a large bowl, mix the mushrooms with all the remaining filling ingredients; reserve.

Preheat the oven to 450°F. To make the sauce, combine the butter and cream in a small pot over medium heat. Cook, stirring occasionally, until cream is slightly reduced. Add all the remaining ingredients and cook, stirring, for 7 minutes. Spread a thin layer of sauce in a rectangular baking dish. Keep the remaining sauce warm.

Lay out a pasta strip. Spread a ¼-inch-thick layer of filling over the entire surface of the strip. Roll up the strip like a jelly roll. With a sharp knife, cut rolled pasta into slices about 1 inch wide. On one cut side of each slice, make 4 slashes, each about ¼ inch deep, in the shape of a cross. Place slices, well spaced, in the sauced baking dish, slashed sides up. Press tops of slices to flare open slightly. Repeat with the remaining strips and filling. Brush slices with butter. Bake on the upper rack of the oven for 15 minutes. Remove from oven and allow to settle for a few minutes before serving.

To serve, form a pool of warm sauce on each of 4 plates. Arrange the roses on the sauce. Garnish each serving with parsley.

SERVES 4.

1 duck (5 pounds)

1 tablespoon kosher salt

2 tablespoons unsalted butter

1 cup sliced fresh shiitake mushrooms

1 large red onion, thinly sliced

12 flour tortillas

1 cup crumbled Stilton cheese

1 bunch fresh cilantro, trimmed

About 2 tablespoons peanut oil

1 cup crème fraîche, for serving

TOMATO SALSA

2 tablespoons finely chopped white onion

2 large tomatoes, coarsely chopped

6 green onions, including some green tops, coarsely
  chopped

3 cloves garlic, finely chopped

2 fresh serrano chiles, seeded, if desired, and finely
  chopped

$\frac{1}{4}$ teaspoon kosher salt

$\frac{1}{4}$ teaspoon freshly ground black pepper

Juice of 1 lime

GUACAMOLE

3 ripe avocados, peeled, pitted, and coarsely chopped

1 tablespoon finely chopped red onion

Juice of $1\frac{1}{2}$ limes

6 dashes Tabasco sauce

2 tablespoons olive oil

$\frac{1}{4}$ teaspoon kosher salt

$\frac{1}{4}$ teaspoon freshly ground black pepper

2 teaspoons finely minced garlic

1 tablespoon finely minced shallots

Shiitake mushrooms and duck in a quesadilla? Why not! It is a combination that has become a big hit at Santacafé. It takes only minutes to prepare once the duck is cooked. Serve this inspired variation on a Southwest classic as an elegant one-course meal.

Preheat the oven to 450°F. Rinse the duck with cold water and pat dry with paper towels. Rub duck, including cavity, with salt. Place duck, breast side up, on a rack in a roasting pan and roast until golden brown, about 1 hour. The duck should be cooked rare. Let cool, then carve meat from carcass, leaving some skin intact if desired. Slice meat into ⅛-inch-thick pieces, about 2 inches long and 1 inch wide.

To make the salsa, in a small bowl combine the white onion, tomatoes, green onions, and garlic; mix gently. Stir in the chiles, salt, pepper, and lime juice. Cover and refrigerate.

To make the guacamole, combine all the ingredients in a medium-sized nonmetallic bowl; toss gently. Cover and refrigerate.

Place a medium-sized skillet over medium-high heat. When skillet is hot, melt the butter and sauté the mushrooms and onion until tender, about 5 minutes.

Preheat the oven to 200°F. Place 1 of the tortillas on a flat surface. Cover with pieces of duck and some of the mushroom-onion mixture. Sprinkle with some of the cheese and cilantro and cover with another tortilla. Assemble 5 additional quesadillas with the remaining ingredients. To cook each quesadilla, heat a steel or cast-iron pan over medium-high heat and add 1 teaspoon of the peanut oil. Slip a quesadilla into the skillet and brown for 2 to 3 minutes on each side. Remove the quesadilla to a heated platter and place in oven until all are cooked.

Cut each quesadilla into wedges and serve with salsa, guacamole, and crème fraîche on the side.

SERVES 6.

1 pound angel hair pasta

1½ cups vegetable stock

2 teaspoons grated fresh ginger

5 cloves garlic, chopped

3 shallots, chopped

5 green onions, chopped

1 dried Chinese chile, finely chopped

¼ cup soy sauce

¼ cup bottled teriyaki sauce

2 tablespoons brown sugar

Juice of 1 orange

⅔ cup water

5 dashes Tabasco sauce

1 tablespoon Chinese black vinegar or red wine
vinegar

2 teaspoons cornstarch, dissolved in 2 tablespoons
water

2 tablespoons Asian sesame oil

Toasted cashews, for garnish

VEGETABLES

2 carrots, peeled and julienned

1 red onion, cut lengthwise into sixths

1 large zucchini, halved lengthwise and thinly sliced
on the diagonal

1 eggplant, thinly sliced and then cut into strips

10 green onions, each trimmed to 5-inch length

1 can (12 ounces) straw mushrooms, drained
(see Note)

1 can (12 ounces) baby corn, drained (see Note)

1 bunch broccoli, stemmed and broken into florets

1 block (about 6 ounces) firm tofu, cut into 1-inch
cubes

The inspiration for this vegetarian dish, which draws upon the kitchens of both Hunan and New Mexico, is the "noodle pillow" I had at Barbara Tropp's famed China Moon restaurant in San Francisco. I prefer De Cecco brand angel hair pasta, but you may use your own favorite high-quality brand. Also feel free to assemble an assortment of vegetables that suits your taste.

Bring a large pot filled with salted water to a boil. Add the pasta and cook until just done. Drain in a colander, rinse under cold water to cool, and drain again. Divide pasta into 8 equal portions. Working quickly, tightly spiral each portion around a long cooking fork. Slide the spiral off the fork onto a flat plate or tray. Repeat with remaining pasta, cover spiraled pillows, and refrigerate.

In a large bowl, combine all of the cut vegetables and tofu; toss vegetables to mix, cover, and refrigerate. The noodles can be formed into pillows and the vegetables can be combined several hours in advance of finishing the cooking.

In a sauté pan over medium-high heat, combine the stock, ginger, garlic, shallots, green onions, and chile and simmer until flavors are blended, about 5 to 7 minutes. Add the soy and teriyaki sauces, sugar, orange juice, water, Tabasco, and vinegar. Bring to a boil, then stir in the cornstarch mixture in a slow, steady stream. Cook, stirring, until sauce is thick enough to coat the back of a spoon, 15 to 20 minutes.

Place 2 large stainless-steel skillets over medium-high heat and heat until very hot. Add 1 tablespoon sesame oil to each skillet and tip skillets to coat the bottoms evenly. Add vegetables to one of the skillets and cook, stirring, until tender but still crisp, about 5 minutes. In the second skillet, place as many pillows as will comfortably fit. Fry until browned, about 4 minutes on each side. Repeat with the remaining pillows.

Arrange the noodle pillows in the center of a heated serving plate and surround with the sautéed vegetables and tofu. Spoon about ¼ cup of the sauce over each pillow, then garnish pillows with cashews.

SERVES *8.*

NOTE: *Canned baby corn and straw mushrooms can be found in Asian markets and well-stocked supermarkets.*

TO END

2 whole eggs

2 egg yolks

½ cup plus 2 tablespoons granulated sugar

6 tablespoons plus 1 teaspoon fresh lemon juice

2 teaspoons freshly grated lemon zest

¼ pound unsalted butter, chilled and cut into 8 pieces

1 cup heavy cream, chilled

2 pints fresh raspberries

6 cups peanut oil, for deep-frying

24 square wonton wrappers (about ½ pound)

½ cup sifted confectioners' sugar

Lemon or orange zest, cut into thin strips, for garnish

I have always loved wonton wrappers and use them in countless ways. I have even used them as a base for tostadas. It occurred to me that a crisply fried wonton wrapper dusted with confectioners' sugar might make a wonderfully light Napoleon. I tried it and loved it.

In a saucepan, whisk together the eggs and egg yolks. Whisk in the ½ cup granulated sugar, the 6 tablespoons lemon juice, and lemon zest. Add the butter pieces all at once and place over medium heat. Cook, stirring constantly, until mixture begins to develop body and thicken, about 4 to 5 minutes. Do not boil. Remove from the heat and pour through a wire-mesh strainer into a bowl. Cover with plastic wrap and refrigerate until chilled.

In a medium-sized bowl, whip the cream until it forms soft peaks. Fold the chilled lemon mixture into the cream. Cover and refrigerate.

Combine the berries, the remaining 2 tablespoons granulated sugar, and the remaining 1 teaspoon lemon juice in a food processor or blender. Process until smooth. Pass through a wire mesh strainer to remove seeds. Cover and refrigerate until ready to serve.

In a large saucepan, heat the oil to 375°F, or until a bit of wonton wrapper turns brown within seconds of being dropped in the oil. Separate wrappers and drop them into the oil, several at a time, frying them until they are golden brown. Remove with a slotted utensil to paper towels to drain. Repeat with the remaining wrappers. When the wrappers are cool, break them into smaller pieces and dust with confectioners' sugar.

To assemble the Napoleons, ladle a pool of the raspberry sauce onto each serving plate. Forming 4 layers in all, alternate broken wontons and spoonfuls of the lemon cream, ending with the cream. Garnish with citrus zest. Serve immediately.

SERVES *8.*

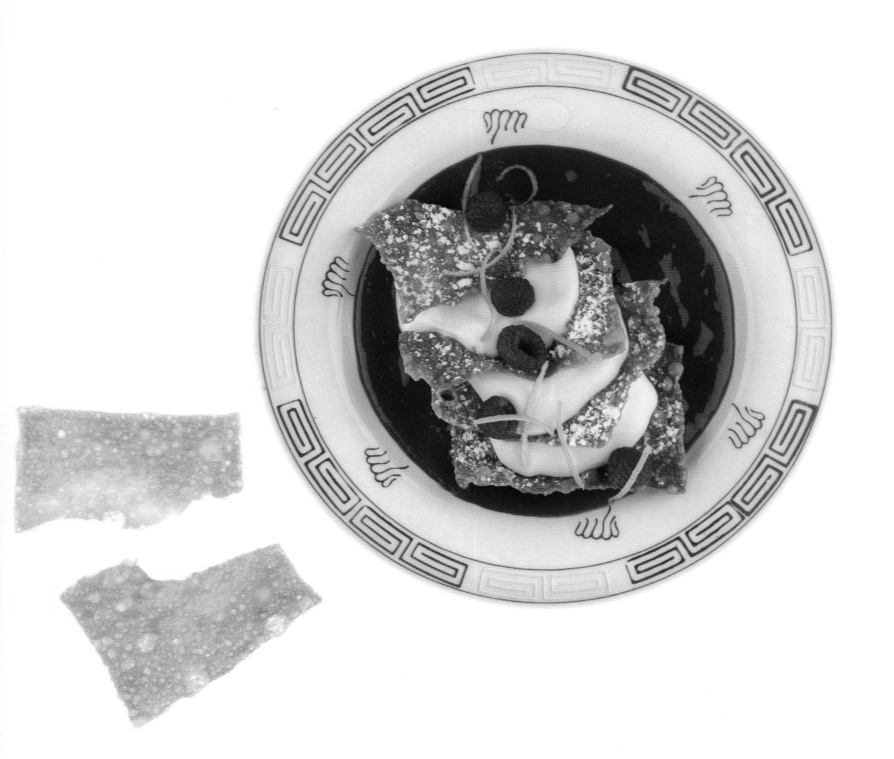

6 ounces fresh ginger

4 cups (1 quart) heavy cream

1 cup sugar

8 egg yolks

Boiling water, as needed

2 ounces candied ginger, for garnish (see Note)

I have tried dozens of flans and their cousins in Spain, Mexico, and Italy. It's amazing how different this classic custard can taste with just a few adjustments in ingredients. Here is my adaptation of a French caramelized custard known as crème brûlée.

Preheat the oven to 300°F. Peel the fresh ginger and thinly slice into ⅛-inch-thick slices. Place ginger slices in a small saucepan and add just enough water to cover. Bring to a boil and boil for 1 minute. Remove from heat and drain off water; reserve ginger.

In a large saucepan, heat the cream over medium-high heat until a film forms on the surface. Remove from heat and add the blanched ginger. Cover and let steep for 30 minutes. Strain and discard the ginger. Reheat the cream and stir in ¾ cup of the sugar until the sugar dissolves.

Place the egg yolks in a bowl. Whisk until well blended. Add 1 cup of the hot cream to the yolk mixture and whisk to mix. Then pour the egg yolk mixture into the remaining cream and whisk together to blend completely. Strain through a fine mesh sieve into a pitcher.

Arrange 8 flameproof, ¾-cup custard dishes in a large baking pan. Evenly distribute the egg mixture among the cups. Pour the boiling water into the baking pan to reach halfway up the sides of the custard dishes. Tightly cover the baking pan with aluminum foil. Bake until the custards are set, about 1 hour. Remove the custards from the pan, cool, cover, and refrigerate for about 2 hours.

Preheat the broiler. Sprinkle 1½ teaspoons of the remaining sugar over the top of each custard. Place custard dishes in the broiler and broil, watching very carefully until the sugar melts and turns golden, 1 to 2 minutes. Serve within 30 minutes or the caramelized sugar will become soggy. Garnish with candied ginger.

SERVES *8.*

NOTE: *Candied ginger is ginger that has been poached in syrup, dried, coated with sugar, and canned. A good substitute is ginger in syrup, sold in glazed green crocks. Both types can be found in Asian markets and some specialty-foods shops.*

1 pound unsalted butter, softened

1 cup sugar

2 eggs

6 cups unbleached flour

1 tablespoon baking powder

$\frac{1}{2}$ teaspoon salt

$\frac{1}{3}$ cup ice water

1 teaspoon vanilla extract

Grated zest of 2 oranges

$\frac{1}{3}$ cup brandy, chilled

Ground cinnamon, for topping

Sugar, for topping

Biscochitos, a traditional New Mexican Christmas treat, are among my favorite cookies—not too sweet and a little spicy. They are great for breakfast with coffee or tea and are also perfect with ice cream.

In a large bowl, cream together the butter and sugar until fluffy. Add the eggs, one at a time, beating well after each addition. Sift together the flour, baking powder, and salt. Gradually add flour mixture to butter mixture, beating well. Add the water, vanilla, orange zest, and brandy; beat just until well combined.

Form dough into a log and cover with plastic wrap. Chill for 30 minutes. Line baking sheets with parchment paper.

On a lightly floured board, roll out chilled dough into a large square about ½ inch thick. Cut square into strips ½ inch wide and 7 inches long. Place strips on prepared sheets. With fingers, curl dough strips into snakelike forms. Dust tops with cinnamon and sugar, cover, and chill for 30 minutes.

Preheat the oven to 350°F. Bake until golden brown, about 10 to 12 minutes. With a long spatula, gently remove cookies to wire racks to cool. Store in an airtight container at room temperature.

MAKES *about 5 dozen cookies.*

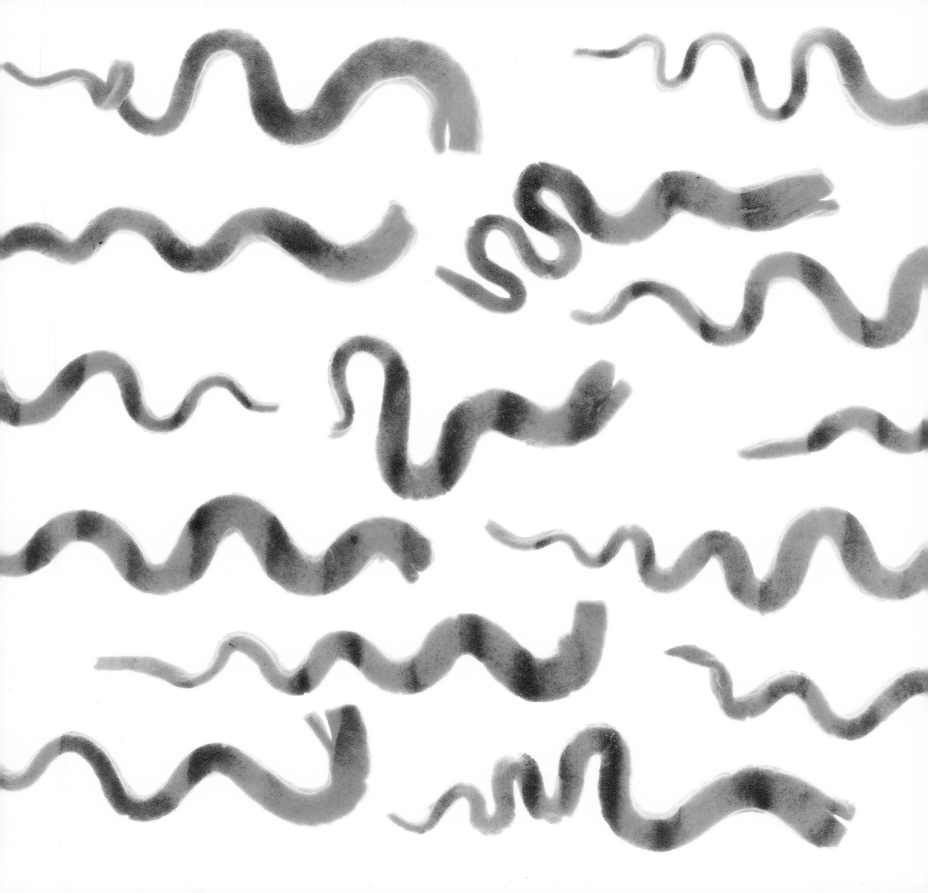

1 pound high-quality imported bittersweet chocolate
½ cup heavy cream
½ cup Japanese plum wine
3 tablespoons unsalted butter
1 cup unsweetened cocoa powder
1 tablespoon ground cinnamon

Hand-formed truffles are easy to make if you are well organized and patient. These delightful spheres are infused with the flavors of Japanese plum wine and cinnamon. Serve with fresh fruit for an even more festive dessert.

Chop the chocolate into small pieces; divide chocolate in half. In the top pan of a double boiler placed over gently simmering water, melt ½ pound of the chocolate. In a small saucepan, heat the cream and add to the melted chocolate. Stir to mix well. Pour the plum wine into a small saucepan and cook over high heat until it is reduced by half. Add the wine and the butter to the chocolate mixture and mix well. Pour the chocolate mixture into a shallow pan so that it forms a sheet 1 inch thick. Cover and chill until set, about 30 to 40 minutes.

Line a baking sheet with parchment paper. Remove the chocolate mixture from the refrigerator. With a small melon baller dipped in very cold water and with cool hands, shape the truffle mixture into balls. Place balls on the prepared baking sheet. Cover and chill again until firm. These balls will become the centers of the truffles.

Place the remaining ½ pound chocolate in the top pan of a double boiler placed over gently simmering water. Stir until completely melted. Remove from heat and continue to stir until the temperature is just warm to the touch (88°F).

Line a second baking sheet with parchment paper. Pick up a chilled chocolate ball and dip it in the melted chocolate. Roll it in the chocolate so that it is completely coated on all sides. Retrieve the truffle with 2 forks and let the excess chocolate drip off. Carefully place the truffle on the prepared baking sheet. Repeat with the remaining chocolate balls. If the melted chocolate becomes too cool for coating, reheat it again; if the truffle centers become too soft, chill them again. Be careful to keep the soft truffle center from melting into the chocolate coating. Let the dipped truffles stand until the chocolate coating has hardened.

Sift together the cocoa powder and cinnamon into a bowl. One by one, place each truffle in the cocoa mixture and gently roll it around to coat completely. Store the truffles in a covered container at room temperature.

MAKES *30 small truffles.*

5 eggs, separated

2 cups plus 5 tablespoons sugar

2 teaspoons vanilla extract

1¼ cups all-purpose flour

½ teaspoon baking powder

Pinch salt

4 pints (1 quart) strawberries

2 lemons

8 ounces fresh ginger, grated

4 cups (1 quart) heavy cream

½ cup sour cream

2 mangoes

Fresh mint sprigs, for garnish

This summer dessert combines sweet fresh strawberries with spicy ginger and whipped cream.

Preheat the oven to 350° F. In a large bowl, combine the egg yolks, ½ cup of the sugar, and vanilla. Whip with an electric mixer on medium speed until pale yellow. Reserve. Sift together the flour and baking powder into a bowl. Whip the egg whites with ½ cup of the sugar and salt until they form stiff, moist peaks. Fold one third of the flour mixture into the whites, then fold in half of the yolk mixture. Fold in half of the remaining flour mixture, followed by all of the remaining yolk mixture. Fold in the remaining flour mixture until just incorporated.

Butter and flour an 11- by 16-inch jelly-roll pan. Pour the batter into the prepared pan and smooth the top. Bake until lightly browned, about 20 minutes. Invert onto a wire rack to cool. Cut cake crosswise into thirds.

Reserve 8 of the whole strawberries for garnish. Place the remaining berries in a saucepan and add 1 cup of the sugar and the juice of 1 lemon. Simmer over medium heat just until the berries have expressed some juice but are still firm. Remove from the heat and strain the juice; reserve. Press out as much juice as possible from half (4 ounces) of the ginger and gently stir into the berries. Cool berries, slice, cover, and refrigerate until ready to use.

In a large bowl, combine the heavy cream, sour cream, and 3 tablespoons of the sugar. Beat until soft peaks form. Cover and refrigerate.

Peel and pit the mangoes; scrape off as much pulp as possible from the peels and pits. Place pulp in a food processor or blender; add the juice of the remaining lemon and purée until smooth. In a small saucepan, combine the purée and the remaining 2 tablespoons sugar. Press as much juice as possible from the remaining 4 ounces of ginger and add to the mango mixture. Simmer over medium heat until flavors are blended, about 5 minutes. Strain through a wire mesh sieve and let cool.

To assemble, place 1 layer of the cake on a board. Brush berry juice over the cake and top layer with half of the sliced berry mixture. Spread one third of the whipped cream mixture over the strawberries and top with the second cake layer. Brush the layer with berry juice, top with the remaining berry mixture, and then spread with half of the remaining cream. Position the third cake layer on top and brush it with berry juice. Spread the remaining cream over the top. Chill for 30 minutes.

To serve, slice cake into 8 squares. Ladle a pool of mango sauce onto each of 8 individual plates. Place a cake square on each plate. Garnish with the reserved whole strawberries and mint.

SERVES *8.*

GINGER ICE CREAM

1 vanilla bean

4 cups (1 quart) heavy cream

8 egg yolks

1 cup sugar

1 cup grated fresh ginger

CAJETA SAUCE

4 cups (1 quart) goat's milk

1½ cups sugar

½ cup light corn syrup

2 sticks cinnamon

1 teaspoon baking soda, dissolved in 1 tablespoon water

The flavor of ginger—a touch of the Orient—distinguishes this new, luxuriously smooth ice cream experience. A ladle of cajeta, *Mexican-style caramel sauce made from goat's milk, adds extra richness.*

To make the ice cream, slice the vanilla bean in half lengthwise with a sharp knife. Combine vanilla bean and 2 cups of the cream in the top pan of a double boiler placed over simmering water. Heat until bubbles form at edge of pan. Remove from heat and set aside. Remove vanilla bean from cream and, with a knife, scrape insides of bean back into the cream; discard pod.

In a large mixing bowl, combine the egg yolks and sugar and beat with an electric mixer on low speed (or by hand) until thick and pale, about 3 minutes. Gradually add half of the heated cream to the yolk mixture, whisking constantly. Add the yolk mixture to the remaining cream in the double boiler. Continue to stir over heat until temperature reaches 178° to 180°F, or until mixture thickens enough to coat the back of a spoon. Remove from heat and let cool. To remove any lumps, strain through a fine mesh sieve.

Press the ginger to extract as much juice as possible and add to the cream mixture. Add the remaining 2 cups cream and stir well. Cover and chill until cold. Freeze in an ice cream maker according to the manufacturer's instructions.

To make the sauce, combine the milk, sugar, corn syrup, and cinnamon sticks in a very large saucepan. Place over medium-high heat and bring to a boil. Remove from heat and stir in baking soda mixture. With a long-handled wooden spoon, stir down to deflate mixture to original volume (the mixture will have bubbled to about 3 times the original volume). Return the saucepan to the heat and bring to a steady rolling boil. Reduce heat and continue to simmer until mixture is a rich caramel color and has the consistency of corn syrup, about 1 hour. It will have reduced to about 2 cups. If desired, cool sauce, cover, and store in the refrigerator. Reheat before serving.

To serve, spoon ice cream into individual serving dishes. Ladle some of the warm sauce over each serving.

SERVES *8 to 10.*

2 eggs

½ cup granulated sugar

1 cup firmly packed brown sugar

¼ cup unsalted butter, melted

2 cups milk

3 cups heavy cream

1½ tablespoons vanilla extract

¼ cup rum

2 ripe pears, peeled, cored, and thinly sliced

½ cup raisins

1 day-old French baguette, cut into ½-inch cubes

Boiling water, as needed

MAPLE SAUCE

½ cup maple syrup

Juice of 1 lemon

2 tablespoons sherry

2 tablespoons water

This old-fashioned pudding with maple sauce and whipped cream is delicious right out of the oven. Any leftovers can be reheated the next day in a warm oven.

Preheat the oven to 350°F. Butter a 4- by 9-inch loaf pan. Line the pan with parchment paper and butter the parchment. In a large bowl, combine the eggs, granulated sugar, ½ cup of the brown sugar, and butter. Add the milk, 2 cups of the cream, vanilla, rum, pears, and raisins. Gently stir in the cubed bread and let stand until moisture is absorbed by bread, about 10 minutes.

Transfer the bread mixture to the prepared loaf pan. Spread the remaining ½ cup brown sugar over the top and cover pan with aluminum foil. Place loaf pan in a larger baking pan and pour boiling water into baking pan to reach halfway up sides of loaf pan. Bake pudding until firm and golden brown, about 1 hour.

Meanwhile, in a medium saucepan, combine all the ingredients for the sauce. Cook over low heat, stirring occasionally, until heated through; keep warm. In a small bowl, whip the remaining 1 cup cream until stiff peaks form; cover and refrigerate until ready to serve.

To serve, remove pudding from oven, remove foil, and cool slightly. Invert pudding onto a wire rack, lift off pan, and peel off parchment paper. Turn pudding upright and cut into slices. Arrange slices on individual plates. Top each serving with a spoonful of warm maple sauce and a dollop of whipped cream.

SERVES *8.*

¾ cup quick-cooking rolled oats

⅔ cup sugar

1 tablespoon all-purpose flour

1 teaspoon baking powder

6 tablespoons unsalted butter, melted

1 egg, lightly beaten

½ teaspoon vanilla extract

8 ounces bittersweet chocolate, chopped in pieces, melted, and stirred until warm to the touch (88°F)

2 ounces white chocolate, chopped in pieces, melted, and stirred until warm to the touch (88°F)

Fresh mint leaves, for garnish

WHITE CHOCOLATE—MINT ICE CREAM

2 cups heavy cream

5 peppermint tea bags

8 egg yolks

1 cup sugar

8 ounces white chocolate, chopped in pieces, melted, and kept warm

2 cups half-and-half cream

2 tablespoons green crème de menthe

This recipe was developed by Stephanie Morris, Santacafé's very creative pastry chef. She recommends using high-quality imported chocolate such as Lindt, Tobler, or Callebaut.

Preheat the oven to 375°F. Line 2 baking sheets with parchment paper and set aside. In a large mixing bowl, combine the oats, sugar, flour, and baking powder; stir to mix thoroughly. Add the butter to the oats mixture and mix to form a moist dough. Add the egg and vanilla and stir to combine thoroughly.

Spoon the dough onto the prepared baking sheets, forming 16 equal portions spaced about 2 inches apart. Smooth and shape the dough into rounds with the back of the spoon. Bake until light brown, about 8 to 10 minutes. Lift the parchment paper with the cookies on it off the hot baking sheets and place on wire racks to cool. Carefully remove cooled cookies from paper with a metal spatula.

To decorate the cookies, dip 8 of the cookies, one at a time, vertically into the melted bittersweet chocolate, thickly coating only half of each cookie. Place on parchment paper and let stand at room temperature until chocolate sets.

Drizzle the melted white chocolate over the tops of the chocolate-dipped cookies, forming a zigzag pattern. Let stand at room temperature until chocolate sets.

To make the ice cream, warm the heavy cream in the top pan of a double boiler placed over simmering water. Add the tea bags, turn the heat off, and let steep.

In a medium-sized bowl, combine the egg yolks and sugar and beat with an electric mixer on low speed (or by hand) until thick and pale, about 3 minutes. Set aside.

Remove tea bags from cream. Reheat cream over simmering water. Gradually add half of the warm cream to the yolk mixture, whisking constantly. Add the yolk mixture to the remaining cream in the double boiler. Continue to stir over heat until temperature reaches 178° to 180°F, or until mixture thickens enough to coat the back of a spoon. Remove from heat. To remove any lumps, strain through a fine mesh sieve. Whisk in warm white chocolate, half-and-half, and crème de menthe. Let cool, cover, and chill for 1 hour. Freeze in an ice cream maker according to the manufacturer's instructions.

For each serving, place a plain cookie on an individual dessert plate and spoon a generous amount of ice cream on top of it. Carefully cap with a chocolate-dipped cookie and very gently press to sandwich ice cream. Garnish with mint leaves.

SERVES *8.*

1⅔ cups all-purpose flour

1¼ cups sugar

Pinch plus ⅛ teaspoon salt

¼ pound plus 5 tablespoons unsalted butter, chilled

1 egg yolk

3 to 4 tablespoons heavy cream

5 whole eggs

2 teaspoons vanilla extract

2 cups dark corn syrup

½ cup rum

2½ cups pecan pieces, toasted

1 cup heavy cream, whipped, for serving

At Santcafé we started out with a recipe for pecan pie and added rum to it. Then we changed the pie to a tart and finally to a deep-dish pie. Here is the recipe for the now-classic Santacafé Deep-Dish Rum-Pecan Pie.

In a large bowl, combine the flour, ½ cup of the sugar, and pinch of salt. Cut the ¼ pound butter into small pieces and add it to the flour mixture. Rub the mixture between your fingertips until it is the consistency of coarse meal. With a fork, stir the egg yolk into the flour mixture. Add the cream, 1 tablespoon at a time, and continue to work the mixture with your fingertips until the dough comes together when pressed between your fingertips. It should not be sticky. Gather the dough into a ball, then flatten it into a disk. Cover with plastic wrap and chill for 1 hour.

Select a 10-inch tart pan with 2-inch sides and a removable bottom. Melt 1 tablespoon of the butter and brush over sides and bottom of pan. Set aside.

Remove dough from refrigerator and let it soften for a couple of minutes. On a lightly floured board, roll out dough, starting from the center and rolling toward the edges until you have a round 16 inches in diameter and ¼ inch thick. Drape the round over the rolling pin and transfer it to the prepared pan. Gently press pastry against the bottom and sides of pan. Fold edges of dough over and gently mold to the pan rim. Cover with plastic wrap and freeze until solid, about 30 minutes.

In a small pan, melt the remaining 4 tablespoons butter; pour into a medium-sized bowl and let cool. Add the remaining ¾ cup sugar and eggs to butter and whisk until the sugar dissolves. Add the remaining ⅛ teaspoon salt, vanilla, corn syrup, and rum; mix until well blended.

Preheat oven to 400°F. Remove pastry shell from freezer and line with aluminum foil all the way up to the rim. Fill the pastry shell with weights or dried beans and bake for 10 minutes. Carefully lift the foil and weights out. Return pastry shell to oven until crust is pale brown, 5 to 10 minutes. Remove from oven and let cool slightly.

Reduce oven temperature to 350°F and fill pastry shell with pecan pieces. Pour corn syrup mixture over nuts. Do not allow filling to drip over edges. Place pie on a baking sheet to catch any drips and bake until filling is set in the middle, about 1 hour. Cool on a wire rack. Serve with whipped cream.

SERVES *8.*

1 package (3 ounces) corn husks

3 large ripe Santa Rosa plums, halved, pitted,
    and coarsely chopped

2 teaspoons ground cinnamon

1 tablespoon granulated sugar

1 teaspoon ground ginger

$\frac{1}{3}$ cup almonds, toasted and coarsely chopped

CORNMEAL DOUGH

$\frac{1}{3}$ cup cornmeal

6 tablespoons *masa harina*

$\frac{1}{2}$ cup plus 2 tablespoons boiling water

4 tablespoons unsalted butter, softened

$\frac{1}{4}$ cup firmly packed brown sugar

$\frac{1}{4}$ cup milk

$\frac{1}{8}$ teaspoon salt

1 teaspoon baking powder

LIME CREAM

2 whole eggs

2 egg yolks

$\frac{1}{2}$ cup granulated sugar

1 tablespoon freshly grated lime zest

$\frac{1}{2}$ cup fresh lime juice

$\frac{1}{4}$ pound unsalted butter, cut into small pieces

In this tantalizing recipe, luscious purple plums and toasted almonds form a tamale filling, which is complemented by a lime-flavored sauce. Place the corn husks in a large saucepan. Add water to cover, bring to a boil, reduce heat, and simmer 10 minutes. Remove from heat, cover, and let stand for 2 hours or refrigerate overnight.

In a large bowl, combine the plums, cinnamon, granulated sugar, ginger, and almonds. Mix well and set aside.

To make the dough, combine the cornmeal, masa harina, and boiling water in a medium-sized bowl. Mix well and let stand for 1 hour. In a large mixing bowl, cream the butter until light colored and fluffy. Add the brown sugar and cornmeal mixture and beat until well blended. Add the milk, salt, and baking powder and continue to beat until mixture is the consistency of cake batter. Set aside.

To make the lime cream, combine the whole eggs, egg yolks, and granulated sugar in a nonreactive saucepan; whisk together until blended. Add the lime zest and juice and mix well. Drop the butter pieces into the egg mixture and place the pan over medium heat. Cook, stirring constantly, until mixture thickens and develops body, about 4 to 5 minutes. Remove from heat and strain through a wire-mesh strainer into a bowl. Cover and refrigerate until ready to serve.

Drain the husks and pat dry. Select 12 of the larger husks. They should be 7 to 8 inches long and 6 inches across on the wide end. Set them aside to use for the tamales. Tear 24 ¼-inch-wide strips from the remaining husks; reserve the strips and the remaining husks.

To form each tamale, lay 1 of the large corn husks on a flat work surface. Evenly spread 3 to 4 tablespoons of the cornmeal mixture on the husk, leaving a 1-inch border on all sides. Then evenly spread 1 tablespoon or so of the plum mixture in the center of the cornmeal layer. Bring the long sides of the husk up to meet; the cornmeal layer should completely enclose the plum filling. Press the edges together and fold them inward to create a lengthwise flap. Twist the open ends closed and loosely tie each end with 1 of the reserved strips.

To steam the tamales, line the rack of a steamer with some of the reserved husks and arrange tamales, folded side down, on the rack. Layer the remaining husks over the tamales. Fill the bottom of the steamer with water and bring it to a boil. Place rack over water, cover with a lid, and steam over gently boiling water for 1½ hours.

To serve the warm tamales, unwrap 1 end of each tamale. Place 2 tamales on each individual serving plate and ladle some of the chilled lime cream over the exposed filling.

ANAHEIM CHILE
A long, narrow, light green chile. It ranges from mild to hot and is the most commonly used chile in the Southwest.

ANCHO CHILE
The name for a dried poblano chile (see Poblano chile). It is a deep red color and usually between 4 and 6 inches long.

ASIAN SESAME OIL
A dark, fragrant oil extracted from roasted sesame seeds. Available in plastic and glass bottles in Asian markets and well-stocked supermarkets.

BELL PEPPER, FRESH, HOW TO ROAST
See Chiles and bell peppers, fresh, how to roast.

BLACK VINEGAR
See Chinese black vinegar.

CHILES
See specific varieties.

CHILES, DRIED, HOW TO ROAST
Dried chiles that form the base of sauces are often roasted and soaked before using. Prepare a fire in a charcoal grill. Rinse dried chiles under cold, running water. Pat dry with a paper towel and remove stems. Slit the chiles open lengthwise and remove seeds and ribs. When coals are red hot, place the chiles on the grill and roast, turning to heat evenly, until lightly toasted. Alternatively, hold the chiles over a gas flame or place under a broiler. Transfer chiles to a bowl and add hot water to cover; let stand 15 minutes. Drain and use as directed in recipes.

CHILES AND BELL PEPPERS, FRESH, HOW TO ROAST
Fresh chiles and bell peppers are often roasted, peeled, seeded, and deribbed before using. Prepare a fire in a charcoal grill. When coals are red hot, place the peppers on the grill and roast, turning to heat evenly, until the skin blisters and chars. Alternatively, hold the peppers over a gas flame or place under a broiler. Transfer peppers to a plastic bag, tightly close the top, and let stand "to sweat" for 5 minutes. Remove peppers from bag and hold under cold, running water. Peel off the skin; it should come off easily. Remove stems and slit the peppers open lengthwise; remove seeds and ribs. Rinse and dry with paper towels before using. Caution: You may want to wear rubber gloves if you have sensitive skin or are handling a lot of chiles.

CHIMAYO CHILE
A medium-hot red chile from the Chimayo region of northern New Mexico that is often dried and ground to a fine powder. If unavailable, use any finely ground red chile.

CHINESE BLACK VINEGAR

Black vinegars are made from wheat or other grains, as well as rice. They generally have a slight bitterness and a great depth of flavor. The black vinegars bottled in Zhejiang, on China's north coast, are particularly fine. Look for black vinegar in Chinese markets.

CHINESE CHILE

Also called Japanese chile. A small, very hot, dried red chile that can be found in Asian markets and some specialty-foods shops.

CORN HUSKS

Dried corn husks are sold by weight or in packages in Latin American markets and well-stocked supermarkets.

CRÈME FRAÎCHE

A cultured cream with a slightly tangy flavor. Somewhat thicker than heavy cream but still pourable, crème fraîche is available in cartons in specialty-foods shops.

ENOKI MUSHROOMS

These creamy-colored mushrooms have long, slender stems and tiny caps. They can be used raw or lightly cooked and are available in Japanese markets and well-stocked supermarkets.

FISH SAUCE

A translucent brown sauce popular throughout Southeast Asia. It is made from small, anchovylike fish or shrimp that have been salted and allowed to ferment in the sun. The resulting liquid is then drained off and bottled. Each country favors a slightly different style of fish sauce; any good-quality sauce bottled in Thailand can be used in the dishes in this book. Fish sauce can be purchased in markets carrying Southeast Asian products and in well-stocked supermarkets.

GARI

Pickled baby ginger that is often served with sushi. Available in plastic containers in Japanese markets and well-stocked supermarkets.

GINGER

Fresh ginger is now available in most markets. The best ginger is very hard, with golden flesh and a greenish tinge to the skin. To store, place ginger in a brown paper bag inside of a plastic bag and keep in the refrigerator.

JALAPEÑO CHILE

A small, bright green, plump chile usually about 2 inches in length. It is very hot and is often pickled to use as a condiment. When ripened, dried, and smoked, it is called chile chipotle.

MASA HARINA

Treated and ground dried corn—used for making tamales and tortillas. Look for masa harina in bags in Mexican markets and well-stocked supermarkets.

NORI

Thin, dried seaweed sheets used in sushi and other rice dishes. For sushi, the nori *should be lightly toasted by holding it over a gas flame until the sheet is lightly crisped (2 or 3 seconds). Look for* nori *in Japanese markets and well-stocked supermarkets.*

PASTA, HOW TO MAKE BY HAND

The pasta recipes in this book call for a food processor and a pasta machine. If you lack this equipment, you can make and roll out the dough by hand. To make the dough, combine the dry ingredients in a large mixing bowl. Make a well in the center and add the wet ingredients to the well. With a fork, gradually combine the dry and wet ingredients, continuing to stir until the mixture forms a mass that holds together. Turn the dough out onto a lightly floured board and knead, then chill as directed for dough made in a food processor. To roll out the dough, lightly flour a work surface. Work with only a small portion of the dough at a time, keeping the remaining dough covered. Roll out the dough, using as few strokes as possible and dusting with flour as necessary to prevent sticking, until the sheet is as thin as a knife blade. Dust the dough with flour and let it rest for 10 to 15 minutes before cutting as directed. If you are making fettuccine or other noodles, roll the dough sheet up into a cylinder, flatten the top slightly, and cut across the roll into ⅛-inch-wide strips. Lift roll so that the noodles hang free, then drape the noodles over a rack or lay them out on a flour-dusted tea towel. Repeat with the remaining dough.

POBLANO CHILE

Dark green and similar in size to a bell pepper, but with a pointed end. The fresh poblano is usually one of the milder chiles, but it can also be very hot. It has a robust flavor and is used for everything from stuffed chiles to soups.

ROASTING CHILES AND BELL PEPPERS

See Chiles and bell peppers, fresh, how to roast.

ROASTING DRIED CHILES

See Chiles, dried, how to roast.

SEASONED RICE VINEGAR

Although rice vinegar is widely used in both Japanese and Chinese cookery, the seasoned rice vinegar called for in this book is a Japanese product. The clear, mild vinegar is lightly seasoned with sugar.

SERRANO CHILE

This slender, piquant green chile is about 2 inches long. It is commonly added to salsas.

SESAME SEED

These tiny seeds are available in two varieties, white and black. White sesame seeds are usually toasted to bring out their full, nutty flavor. To toast, place the seeds in a dry skillet over moderate heat and, shaking the skillet to prevent burning, heat until seeds are a warm brown and very fragrant. Black sesame seeds are used untoasted.

SHIITAKE MUSHROOM

Cultivated fresh shiitake mushrooms are now available in many regions of the United States. Sometimes called black forest mushrooms or Chinese black mushrooms, these thick-capped, deep brown mushrooms are gathered in the wild as well as cultivated in Japan, Korea, and China. In the former two countries they are used both fresh and dried; the Chinese traditionally use them dried. Fresh shiitake mushrooms can be stir-fried, grilled, or steamed.

SICHUAN PEPPERCORNS

Also known as wild pepper and anise pepper. These are not peppercorns at all. They are dried brown berries that are native to western China but are used in cooking throughout the country. Look for Sichuan peppercorns in cellophane bags in Chinese markets.

SQUID OR CUTTLEFISH INK

Available at select gourmet shops, frozen in small packets. On several occasions I have tried to remove the ink from the ink sacs of squid. I find it extremely difficult and recommend that you buy it instead.

TAMARI

A fermented soybean product that is very similar to soy sauce but stronger in flavor. It is available in bottles in natural-foods shops and Japanese markets.

TERIYAKI SAUCE

A blend of soy sauce, sugar, mirin (rice cooking wine), and sake that is often used for marinating and glazing grilled meats. The sauce is available in bottles in Japanese markets and many supermarkets.

THAI CHILE

Similar to the serrano chile, this slender, small chile is very hot. It is used in curries and sauces and is available green, red, or dried. Thai chiles are often available frozen in Southeast Asian markets. Serrano chiles may be substituted.

TOFU

The Japanese name for a processed creamy white soybean product that is available in soft and firm forms. Also marketed as bean curd, tofu is cut into blocks and packaged in water in plastic containers. The soft form is generally used in soup; the firm form can be cut in pieces and used in stir-fries and other dishes. To fry soft tofu, press it under a weight for an hour or so to remove excess moisture, then drain well before using.

WASABI

This is the product of an aquatic root with pale green flesh. The root is grated to form a fine powder, which is then mixed with just enough tepid water to produce the hot, smooth horseradishlike paste that traditionally accompanies sushi. Wasabi powder can be purchased in cans in Japanese markets and well-stocked supermarkets.

WONTON WRAPPERS

Thin wheat wrappers either square or round and usually measuring about 3½ inches square or in diameter and ¹⁄₁₆ inch thick. They can be found wrapped in plastic in 1-pound packages in the cold case of Chinese markets and in well-stocked supermarkets. (Gyoza wrappers, which are used to make Japanese dumplings, may be substituted when round wrappers are needed.) The number of wrappers per package will vary, from 40 up to 80 and more, depending upon the manufacturer. Store any leftover wrappers, well wrapped, in the refrigerator for up to a week.